Prospective Ergonomics

Human-Machine Interaction Set

coordinated by
Jérôme Dinet

Volume 4

Prospective Ergonomics

André Liem

WILEY

First published 2017 in Great Britain and the United States by ISTE Ltd and John Wiley & Sons, Inc.

ISTE Ltd
27-37 St George's Road
London SW19 4EU
UK

www.iste.co.uk

John Wiley & Sons, Inc.
111 River Street
Hoboken, NJ 07030
USA

www.wiley.com

© ISTE Ltd 2017

The rights of André Liem to be identified as the author of this work have been asserted by him in accordance with the Copyright, Designs and Patents Act 1988.

Library of Congress Control Number: 2017948830

British Library Cataloguing-in-Publication Data
A CIP record for this book is available from the British Library
ISBN 978-1-78630-256-4

Contents

Preface

My motivation to write this book on strategic design and prospective ergonomics (PE) has been driven by more than 20 years of experiences as an educator, researcher and design practitioner.

As user needs become increasingly complex, I stress the importance of strategic management for PE and strategic design. Forces of globalization, the proliferation of multicultural societies and emphasis on user experiences have changed the ergonomic, business and design landscape. The concept of "user experience", with respect to products and services, whether in terms of purely use, ownership or a combination of it, has become a topic of debate among designers, ergonomists, user interaction experts, business management and social science authorities.

Moreover, the significant growth of new technologies has revolutionized the way firms use these technologies both internally and externally to improve operations, increase efficiencies and provide functional benefits for customers. For example, in the service industry, providers and retailers are using a wide range of self-service technologies, including the internet, to allow customers to produce and consume services electronically without direct contact from firm employees [MEU 00]. At present and in the future, these new technologies will continue to challenge the different stakeholders, who are engaged in "innovation"; a process of transforming an idea or invention into a good or service that creates value for customers (www.businessdictionary.com).

However, when adopting a more sustainable and altruistic perspective toward innovation, the discrepancy between technology-driven positivism and the desired role of technology in society can be perceived as one of the largest paradoxes of our time.

In this book, I attempt to develop a prospective ergonomic framework to structure and connect generic strategies [WHI 01], worldviews and modes of design reasoning. As exemplified in Whittington's perspectives on strategizing[1], I have been convinced during these years that the main objectives in business and design are broader than just profit maximization and sales. Different stakeholders have diverse ambitions and interests, and designers are creating new roles for themselves in response to new industrial and societal challenges. The current attention on designing experiences, whether tangible or intangible, has placed a significant emphasis on human-centered and design-driven approaches, methods and tools.

Within the polarities of deliberate versus emergent "processes" and targeted versus plural "outcomes", I am convinced that strong similarities between generic strategies and modes of design reasoning can be identified, which may justify a typical ergonomic or design intervention. For example, a classical approach in strategizing resembles a problem solving approach in designing. Both activities are based upon deliberate processes and outcomes are in terms of management "profit maximization", whereas in design it is about "solving a design problem". Furthermore, similarities between design and strategic management/innovation are noticeable in the transient application of methods and tools. For example, visual tools, which are predominantly assistive in projecting an imaginary vision of the future, can be applied in both fields. In other words, the convergence of strategizing perspectives and modes of design reasoning, complemented by their methods and tools brings us to the core of "prospective ergonomics", which is characterized by its anticipative and imaginary nature [ROB 09].

In this work, I argue for a prospective turn in ergonomics to challenge the established fields of strategic design and management. Differences, similarities and relationships between strategic design and PE are being reviewed using existing theories and frameworks from design, ergonomics, strategic and innovation management. PE has developed from corrective and

---

1 Whittington's generic strategy framework is an important element in my thesis. In conjunction with the evaluation of selected worldviews and models of design reasoning, it provides a foundation for discussing different ergonomic and design interventions. Furthermore, the axial dimensions of Whittington's framework, which are "Process *(deliberate versus emergent)*" and "Outcome *(Plural versus specific)*", also form the basis for positioning the selected worldviews as well as modes of design reasoning.

preventive ergonomics to be more "forward looking in time" by emphasizing on context, user-experience and human-centeredness. In terms of practice, PE creates awareness among actors that the anticipation of user needs and imagination of radically new products and services are essential for the survival of organizations, their business ecosystems, and formation of societal contexts. The latter encourages PE to adopt stances and reinvent social contexts, which have been impacted by technological advancement and disruptive innovation. Considering the complex constellation of collaborators and context embeddedness in specific design and development projects, PE interventions particularly support innovation activities, which capitalize on deliberate processes by making use of prescriptive methods and tools as well as by aiming for pluralistic results. In the first instance, this book presents several theoretical frameworks to discern the relationship between PE and SD, built upon existing business management and innovation theories. To complement the theoretical part, 12 cases have been organized and analyzed in greater depth according to four main dimensions of analysis. These dimensions were as follows: (1) orientation, (2) type of design reasoning models they were subjected to, (3) their significance for practice, and finally (4) their value contribution to society and stakeholders. Furthermore, cross comparisons were made based upon these dimensions of analysis and reference to how these cases were positioned according to a generic strategy framework. From an educational perspective, results have implicated how design knowledge and skills should be transferred to students. Namely, a hermeneutic, reflective and participatory mode of designing, supported by a constructivist worldview, requires a mentorship and scholarship approach in research- or practice-based learning. In the discussion and conclusion sections, outcomes from individual cases as well as their cross-comparisons have been taken into account by theoretical frameworks in answering five research questions. These outcomes have indicated that innovating through a PE approach is about finding the right balance between, on the one hand, meeting primary objectives, such as profit maximization or solving the design problem, and, on the other hand, achieving social and human well-being, personal interest and ambitions, family relations, etc. Moreover, intervention of PE within a classical strategy perspective requires organizations to couple push–pull market strategies while considering the interest of different stakeholders throughout all stages of the development process. This means that prescriptive approaches, methods and tools in the positivist mode should be complemented with constructive modes of reasoning and designing as well as reflective methods and tools, while taking into consideration all levels and perspectives of value creation.

In future research, I suggest developing sustainable product-service innovation, business and design strategies to become more pluralistic and contextually embedded in nature, whether deliberate or emergent. Involving the participation of a broad network of stakeholders, these strategies are to be applied to selected key areas such as (1) processes, methods and tools, (2) perspectives and mindsets and (3) challenges pertaining to typical focal areas within the context of PE. Identified focal areas are (1) aesthetics and experience design, (2) transportation design, (3) culture, acculturation and interaction design, (4) service design, (5) inclusive design and (6) healthcare and welfare design.

To further elaborate on the above, providing organizations with an understanding of the situated context and dynamic interaction among stakeholders is more important than helping them to positivistically aim for precise, logical and rational innovations and designs. This can be established by creating awareness among researchers, ergonomists and designers that constructivist, reflective and hermeneutic methods and practices are increasingly taking center stage in PE. Moreover, the need for more prominent constructive approaches has been instigated by a change in outlook from different actors in business settings to be more pluralistic oriented, as well as emerging trends and developments in the areas of sustainable product and service design, welfare technologies, corporate social responsibility, etc.

On a personal note, based upon my technical educational background in industrial design engineering (TU Delft), and my current employment at the Norwegian University of Science and Technology, Department of Product Design, I am predominantly approaching and writing this book from a positivistic and structured perspective. However, having frequent interactions with other non-engineering institutions in design teaching and research has guided me to adopt a broader perspective toward designing and design processes, acknowledging and promoting reflective, hermeneutic and participative modes of thinking through more constructivist worldviews.

André LIEM

August 2017

1

Perspectives and Transitions in Ergonomics

In this chapter, a historical introduction as well as an overview of the present and prospective developments of ergonomics will be given. The aim is to provide an outline for approaching theory building within prospective ergonomics (PE), which in Chapters 2 and 3 will be aligned with ancillary fields of strategic design, innovation, systems and industrial design. To contextualize the work, a range of design approaches, such as systems design, design driven and human/user-centered design, will be introduced with respect to different ergonomic perspectives.

Moreover, this chapter sets the tone for developing the construct of prospection and prospective ergonomics by arguing that this new field of ergonomics is driven by a focus on well-being, by being future oriented and design driven and by the fact that product-service innovation, performance and profit should be sought after within systematically embedded contexts. From this perspective of prospection, the intention is to contextually bring the study of preventive and corrective ergonomics closer to the fields of design and strategic management. Consequences are that with the proliferation of services, human–product interactions and sustainable design, where innovation is usually a concern of many stakeholders, the field of preventive ergonomics is extended to PE and design to strategic design. To conclude this introductory chapter as well as initiate the formation and application of theoretical frameworks, it has been brought forward that pluralism toward the creation of new products and services is a typical trait of PE, which enhances company's competitive advantage.

1.1. History and definition of ergonomics

Ergonomics is the scientific discipline investigating the interaction between humans and artifacts and the design of systems where people participate. It applies systematic methods and knowledge about people to evaluate and approve the interactions between individuals, technology and organizations at work and during leisure. The purpose of design activities is to match systems, jobs, products and environments to the physical and mental abilities and limitations of people [HEL 97]. The aim is to create a working environment (as far as possible) that contributes to achieving healthy, effective and safe operations.

The study of ergonomics (Gr. ergon + nomos) was originally defined and proposed by the Polish scientist Jastrzebowski in 1857, as a scientific discipline with a very broad scope and a comprehensive range of interests and applications, encompassing each human activity, including labor, entertainment, reasoning and dedication [KAR 05]. A historical overview of ergonomics will be presented in the textbox below to make certain events explicit, where business strategies, the design of products and services, and different ergonomic interventions connect. The historical timeline indicates that ergonomics has engaged in systemic ways of strategizing as early as the beginning of 20th Century ergonomics. However, only in the past 25 years has ergonomics gained acceptance among business managers.

According to Perrow [PER 83], the problem of ergonomics is that too few ergonomists work in companies, that they have no control over budgets and people, and that they are seen solely as protectors of workers, rather than creators of products, systems and services. Presently, the value of ergonomics extends beyond occupational health and safety and related legislation. While maintaining health and safety of consumers and workers, ergonomics has become more valuable in supporting company's business strategies to stay competitive. This has led to the acceptance of the following broader definition of ergonomics:

– ergonomics (or human factors) is a scientific discipline, which aims to develop an understanding about the interaction between humans and other system elements. Furthermore, the profession applies theory, principles, data and design methods to optimize human well-being and overall system performance [IEA 00];

– compared to Jastrzebowski's definition, the field of ergonomics has become more proactive with respect to problem solving, design, functional usability and the planning of innovative products and services [ROB 09]. Given this emphasis on ergonomics, the link between business strategies and ergonomics is being established through their common interest in creating and designing improved or new products. Companies are increasingly aware that innovation is essential for maintaining a competitive advantage. As all innovations start with a creative idea [AMA 96], which is both novel and suited to the context of the task [BON 09], it has been acknowledged that end-users of products and services can be important resources for product design and innovation [KRI 02, VON 86]. Within the traditions of preventive ergonomics, user involvement is considered essential for the development of user-friendly product and services, and the participatory design methods and tools that have been developed could be useful for linking ergonomics with product and service innovation.

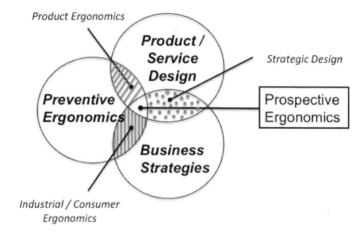

Figure 1.1. *Interaction among product and service design, business strategies and preventive ergonomics toward prospective ergonomics*

Nowadays ergonomics in industry has the dual purpose of promoting both productivity and "well-being" during and related to working conditions. The continuous search for an optimized balance between productivity and favorable working conditions has given rise to a relatively new type of ergonomics, which is "prospective ergonomics". The focus of this work is to promote a "prospective turn" to ergonomics as an important feature in strategy formulation and innovation. This means that attention to PE and strategic design can be an important element of how a company realizes its competitive advantage. Figure 1.1 depicts how the interaction between product and service design, business strategies and preventive ergonomics as an emergent field of ergonomics, namely PE, could be envisioned. Consequently, PE redefines the ergonomic profession to be more design and business oriented. However, with its original focus on human well-being and anticipation of hidden future needs, the business orientation of PE is pluralistic rather than being purely driven by performance and profit maximization. In practice, this means that the ergonomist must consider the dynamic context of the firm and understand the different strategic objectives of stakeholders [DUL 09].

A historical overview of ergonomics

In the 18th Century, Ramazinni published "The diseases of workers", where he documented the connection between occupational hazards and different types of work performed. For example, he described how repetitive hand motions, constrained body posture and excessive mental stress caused cumulative trauma disorders.

At the beginning of the industrial revolution, LaMettrie published a controversial piece of work: L'homme Machine (1748), where he outlined that differences in machine and human capabilities are sensitive, and that one can learn much about human behavior by considering how machines operate. For example, the comparison of robots and humans has facilitated our understanding of how industrial tasks should be designed to fit humans better [HEL 95]. According to Rosenbrock [ROS 83], the concept of human-centered design was introduced as early as the industrial revolution through tools, such as spinning machines (spinning mule) used to spin cotton and other fibers. The aim was to allocate interesting tasks to the human operator, but let the machine handle repetitive ones.

The emphasis in ergonomics at the beginning of the 20th Century was largely attributed to Frederick Taylor's "scientific study of work". However, his name and work have negative connotations and provoke strong reactions from labor unions and worker's welfare organizations. In the period round 1900, Taylor examined and scrutinized in what is called the "Taylor system", how activities were carried out, what movements people made and how much time it took them using time and motion studies. Next, he determined how productivity can be optimized by executing all operations as effectively as possible as in the

---

minimum amount of time, which resulted in rushed systems, assembly line production, etc.

In the same tradition, Frank and Lillian Gilbreth developed time and motion studies to divide ordinary jobs into several small microelements, called "therbligs" [KON 92]. These objections against Taylorism have resulted in much research to select, classify and train human operators from a well-being rather than productivity perspective. Rejecting the element of exploitation, the current focus is on ergonomics design of environments and artifacts, which means "fitting the task to the person", not "fitting the person to the task".

Ergonomics emerged as a scientific discipline in the 1940s because of the growing realization that most people were not able to understand and use the equipment to its full potential and exploits its benefits, as technical equipment became increasingly complex. Focusing on the well-being of workers and manufacturing productivity, the field started to engage in industrial applications in the 1950s and has used information and concepts from work physiology, biomechanics and anthropometry for designing workstations and processes.

As the discipline evolved, variations in terminology emerged in different countries. In the United States, the term human factors took on the same meaning as ergonomics in the UK and continental Europe. Although both terms have been and remain synonymous to professionals, popular usage has somehow nuanced the meaning of the terms. Human factors study the cognitive areas of the discipline (perception, memory, etc.), whereas ergonomics specifically deals with physical aspects, such as workplace layout, light, heat, noise, etc. This is exemplified by how the terms human factors engineering, human factors and engineering psychology has proliferated in the United States military sector after WWII, where high demands were placed on the physical and cognitive demands of the human operator. Many military design problems were encountered in the use of sophisticated war equipment, such as airplanes, radar and sonar stations, and tanks. For example, during the WWII, with the increasing number of pilots and technological complexity of airplanes, it was discovered that cockpits were not adequately and logically organized and designed, causing fatal accidents to occur.

In Europe, technological achievements of WWII and post-WWII were quickly transferred to civilian applications, including the design of consumer products such as cars and computers. Here, similar problems of disharmony between people and equipment were encountered. This resulted in poor user performance and an increased risk of human error. Particularly in Germany, The Netherlands and across Scandinavia the foundation for ergonomics was developed out of medical and functional anatomy studies, while in Eastern Europe growth was largely from the industrial engineering profession [SIN 94].

Thereafter, the Ergonomics Research Society (ERS), which was founded in 1949 from a theoretical and research perspective, has evolved to represent the current discipline, both in the United Kingdom and internationally. In 1977, the ERS was renamed the Ergonomics Society (ES), because of an increased focus on the professional practice and application of ergonomics. The ES became the first professionally registered body and Charity in the field of ergonomics. It also gained the status of a Company limited by guarantee in 1985.

1.2. Classification and positioning of ergonomics

Over the past 50 years, ergonomics has evolved as a unique and independent discipline that focuses on the nature of human–artifact interactions, and made connections with engineering, design, technology and management from a science perspective. Within a systemic human–artifact relationship, a variety of natural and artificial products, processes and living environments are emphasized [KAR 05].

The analysis of poor performance, human errors and accidents due to difficulties faced by the human operator when interacting with objects in specific contexts provided a growing body of evidence to facilitate the understanding of man–machine systems (now human–machine systems) and interactions. This stimulated research by the ergonomic academic and military community which led to further investigations of the interactions between people, equipment and their environments. Accordingly, this has resulted in a substantial body of documented knowledge, methodologies and skills for analyzing and designing interactive systems between humans and their environment [DUL 12]. When defining ergonomics from a practice perspective, ergonomic practitioners continue to improve tasks, jobs, products, technologies, processes, organizations, environments and systems to make them compatible with the needs, abilities and limitations of people through planning, design, implementation, evaluation and redesign [IEA 00].

Contemporary ergonomics shows rapidly expanding application areas, continuing improvements in research methodologies, and increased contributions to fundamental knowledge as well as important applications fulfilling the needs of the society at large and its environment. The environment is usually complex and consists of the physical environment ("things"), the organizational environment (how activities are organized and controlled) and the social environment (other people, culture) [MOR 00, WIL 00, CAR 06]. Fundamental characteristics of contemporary ergonomics are that it takes a systems approach, that it is design driven and that it focuses on two related outcomes: performance and well-being.

Building upon the concept of contemporary ergonomics, a relatively new type of ergonomics, which is "prospective ergonomics (PE)" will be introduced with respect to other areas of ergonomics. In the first instance, a structural and systematic depiction of different classifications of ergonomics is shown in Table 1.1 based upon domain, intervention, focus and specialization. Thereafter, Figure 1.2 will show the positioning of PE as well as its connectivity with strategic and industrial design, and with respect to the other ergonomic interventions.

Domain	Product ergonomics		Industrial ergonomics
Intervention	Corrective ergonomics	Design ergonomics	Prospective ergonomics
Focus	Microergonomics	Mesoergonomics	Macroergonomics
Specialization	Physical ergonomics	Cognitive ergonomics	Organizational ergonomics

Table 1.1. *Classification of ergonomics according to domain, intervention, focus and specialization*

1.2.1. *Ergonomics classified according to domain*

Broadly speaking, the domain of ergonomics can be divided into "Product" and "Industrial". Product ergonomics is a subset of ergonomics, which addresses people's interaction with products, systems and processes. The emphasis within product ergonomics is to ensure that designs complement the strengths and abilities of people to minimize the effects of their limitations. As a result of this, it becomes necessary to understand variabilities represented in the populations, with respect to age, size, strength, cognitive ability, prior experience, cultural expectations and goals.

Researchers and practitioners study how people, on a daily basis, interact with products, processes and environments to make them safer, more comfortable, easier to use and more efficient. They apply relevant research on biomechanical, physiological and cognitive aspects and juxtapose them with knowledge and understanding of the users and their experiences (*Human Factors and Ergonomics: hfes.org, website accessed 2014*).

Industrial ergonomics analyzes information about people, job tasks, equipment and workplace design to assist employers in generating a safe and productive environment for their employees. They emphasize the adaptation of job tasks to human ability within work settings such as those found in manufacturing, engineering and construction. On a more formal note, research encompasses how ergonomics influences or is influenced by job design, health and safety management, training, automation and process optimization, etc. [LUS 14].

1.2.2. *Ergonomics classified according to intervention*

With respect to intervention, corrective, preventive and prospective ergonomics are topics that will be discussed in this section. De Montmollin [DE 67] has categorized ergonomics into corrective ergonomics and preventive/design ergonomics. The former is about correcting existing artifacts, and the latter deals with systems that do not yet exist. According to Laurig [LAU 86], "corrective ergonomics" is associated with traditional ergonomics and is described as developing "corrections through scientific studies". In this context, "developing corrections" refers to situations where the ergonomist or designer makes user and functional improvements to existing products, systems or processes in a reactive manner; in other words: "redesigning".

Furthermore, Robert and Brangier [ROB 09] have mapped out the differences and similarities among corrective, preventive/design and prospective ergonomics. Comparisons across the three subsets of interventions, which are interesting when aligned with a similar comparison within design and strategic design later on, are:

– nature of work and intervention with respect to temporality and expected outcomes;

– main focus and starting point for human factors activities;

– implications for research and data collection.

Nelson *et al.* [NEL 12] proposed aligning the product development process with different ergonomic interventions, as shown in Figure 1.2. Developed around speculative scenario building, PE is strongly compared with framing "use" based on a given design brief. From this prospective ergonomic perspective, scenarios are intended to assist decision making at three main stages in the design process [ROS 02]: (1) the analysis of problem situations in the start of the process, (2) the generation of design solutions at various levels of complexity and (3) the evaluation of these design decisions according to User-centered Design (UCD) criteria. In this context, it can be argued that the purpose of scenarios in the early stages of design is not only to provide an accurate vision of future user activity, but also to crystallize designers' current knowledge and assumptions about future activity. Thus, from this point of view, scenarios of future use in PE are not just a material for analysis, but also a product of creative design [NEL 14]. However, there is ample potential to implement PE thinking much earlier in the design process. For instance, from a strategic design perspective, PE can be introduced in the Fuzzy-Front-End of Innovation to intervene in product planning and goal finding activities, where future product and/or service proposals are sought after.

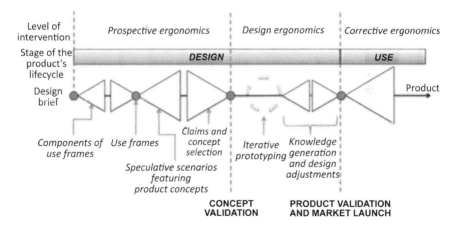

Figure 1.2. *Alignment of the product development process with different ergonomic interventions (adopted from [NEL 12, p. 9])*

1.2.3. *Ergonomics classified according to focus*

In terms of "focus", ergonomics can be classified into micro-, meso- and macroergonomics. Macroergonomics can be perceived as a top-down approach to study sociotechnical developments respective to the design and application of an overall work system involving human–job, human–machine and human–software interfaces [HEN 86, HEN 01]. Dray [DRA 85] defines macroergonomics as a three-generation paradigm: (1) user–machine interface, (2) group–technology interface and (3) organization–technology interface.

This top-down approach implies a transient relationship between macro and microergonomics. The first two paradigms are mainly aligned with microergonomics, whereas "organization–technology interface" is typically a phenomenon to be addressed by macroergonomics. Hereby, the concept of human–centeredness is being emphasized, as the worker's professional and psychosocial characteristics are being considered in the design of a work system. Subsequently, the work system design is being realized through the ergonomic design of specific jobs and related hardware and software interfaces [ROB 01]. Integral to this human-centred design process is the humanized task approach in allocating functions and tasks to collaborative design of technical and personnel subsystems. At an organization-technology interface level, participatory ergonomics is a primary methodology of macroergonomics involving employees at all organizational levels in the design process [IMA 86].

Effective macroergonomic design drives several aspects of the microergonomic design of the work system and makes sure that system components are properly aligned and compatible with the work system's overall structure. This sociotechnical approach enables technical and personnel subsystems to be jointly optimized from top to bottom throughout the organization as well as harmonized with the work system's elements and external environments [HEN 91]. When overarching systems, subsystems and system elements are properly aligned and coordinated, it may lead to increased productivity, better quality and improved employee safety, well-being and health, such as psychosocial comfort, motivation and perceived quality of work life [ROB 01].

With respect to complex human–machine systems as well as sociotechnical system concepts, Emery and Trist [EME 60] perceive organizations as open systems, engaged in transforming inputs into desired outputs, and whose permeable boundaries are exposed to the environments in which they exist and upon which they are dependent for their survival. This management perspective toward different orientations of innovation, use of methods, practices and value creation forms the context for strategic design and prospective ergonomic thinking, involving various communities and stakeholders. In other words, the issue of permeability, which concerns unrestricted transfer of knowledge and practices across different levels of value creation, provides interesting avenues for the development of reasoning approaches, processes, methods and tools, which can be applied in PE and strategic design.

1.2.4. *Ergonomics classified according to specialization*

Traditionally, specialization within ergonomics can be classified according to physical, cognitive and organizational ergonomics. Physical ergonomics is primarily concerned with the human anatomy, studying anthropometric, physiological and biomechanical characteristics related to physical activities [CHA 93, PHE 86, KRO 94, KAR 99, NRC 01]. In cognitive ergonomics, mental processes such as perception, memory, information processing, reasoning and motoric response are a focal point of study, because they are instrumental in determining interactions between humans and ancillary system elements [VIC 99, HOL 03, DIA 04]. Organizational ergonomics, which is similar to macroergonomics, deals with how organizational structures, policies and processes can be optimized within the context of sociotechnical systems [REA 99, HOL 03, NEM 04]. The optimization of human well-being, and overall systems performance, includes the following topics: communication, crew resource management, design of working times, teamwork, participatory work design, community ergonomics, computer-supported cooperative work, new work paradigms, virtual organizations, telework and quality management [KAR 98].

To conclude this chapter, the various ways one is able to classify human factors show that the field has advanced significantly. According to Norman [NOR 10], "The field of Human Factors and its many descendants – Cognitive Engineering, Human-Computer Interaction, Cognitive Ergonomics, Human-Systems Integration, etc. – has made numerous, wonderful advances in the many decades since the enterprise began". However, the discipline still serves many to rescue rather than to create. "It is time for a change".

1.3. A systems approach in ergonomics

According to Merriam Webster, a system is an integrated compilation of interacting and interdependent components (accessed October 7, 2015). Within the context of ergonomics, adopting a system- and design-driven approach in the development of products and services establishes a broader understanding of how a strategic prospective ergonomic approach contributes to performance, well-being and stakeholder involvement [DUL 12].

Ergonomics focuses on the design of these systems consisting of humans and their environment [HEL 97, SCH 09]. The system consists of the human-made elements, for example (work)places, tools, products, technical processes, services, software, built environments, tasks and organizations as well as other humans [WIL 00]. An ergonomic system approach addresses issues on various levels: micro, meso and macro. A microergonomic system approach level is concerned with how humans use tools or perform single tasks, whereas at a mesolevel, humans are considered a part of technical processes or organizations. At a macrolevel, humans are perceived as an element in networks of organizations, regions, countries or the world [RAS 00, DUL 12].

This interdisciplinary systems approach, which has its roots in engineering, is becoming even more important, when ergonomic expertise is redirected to discover prospective hidden needs of various user populations and stakeholders. Furthermore, as positivistic inclined systems engineers advocate the application of technical design specifications as the true basis for the product design, ergonomists' expertise complements such systems approaches from a human-centered perspective to directly impact the work of the design and development team as well as the final design of the product. To be more specific, impact can occur from a hardware ergonomic perspective, software ergonomic perspective, environmental ergonomic perspective and macroergonomic perspective [SAM 05]. This implies that when engineers, designers and ergonomists define problems and formulate solutions within the broader context of the human in a prospective context, system boundaries need to be clearly defined, and be more focused on people specific aspects (e.g. only physical), specific aspects of the environment (e.g. only workplace) or a specific level (e.g. micro).

1.4. Design-driven versus a human-centered approach

In the design process, micro-, meso- and macrolevel ergonomics should be understood from a human component perspective, covering individual, collective and social aspects. Given these foci, ergonomic specialists and interpreters [VER 08] are expected to become more actively involved in creation processes, particularly with respect to the design of product service systems (PSS). Furthermore, actors, who will be part of the system being designed, are often brought into the development process as participants [NOR 91]. All stakeholders' insights and competencies regarding methods for designing and assessing technical and organizational environments, analyzing and acting on situations, and methods for organizing and managing participatory approaches are invaluable for continuously improving PSS [WOO 00].

With respect to PE, designers, ergonomist and participative users should adopt an integrative role in collective design decision making with other contributors and stakeholders of design [RAS 00] based on their knowledge, activities, needs and skills. Furthermore, in the process of analyzing, contextualizing and managing design problems, PE has the legitimacy to stimulate and moderate design processes by, for instance, translating engineering terminology or concepts to end-user terminologies and vice versa.

1.5. Focus on performance and well-being

Three related system outcomes can be achieved by fitting the environment to the human: well-being (e.g. health and safety, pleasure, learning, personal satisfaction and development), performance (e.g. productivity, efficiency, effectiveness, quality, innovativeness, flexibility, systems) and safety (security, reliability, sustainability). Especially within the context of PE and strategic design, it is a challenge for ergonomists to balance multiple outcomes, such as well-being, exposure to learning and profit maximization. In other words, ergonomists need to manage practical implications and ethical trade-offs within systems [WIL 09], considering short- and long-term interdependency between performance and well-being.

This interdependency between performance and well-being is an issue that needs to be aligned[1] with strategic business principles. Once aligned and

---

1 The concept of "aligning" is comparative and based on contemporary perspectives and theoretical frameworks rather than tracing back historical events.

understood, looking at prospection can advance a proactive design approach within ergonomics. In other words, the expansion from traditional to contemporary ergonomics has promoted the concept of "prospection" and introduced a new framework for structuring ergonomic activities around corrective, preventive (design) and PE [BRA 10, ROB 12]. The latter looks forward in time defining human needs and activities to create human-centered artifacts that besides their usefulness provide positive user experiences. Figure 1.3 shows the various dimensions determining PE, which extend beyond well-being, productivity and a system approach. It stresses the importance of being future oriented, pluralistic and emphasizes that innovative design solutions are systemically embedded in context.

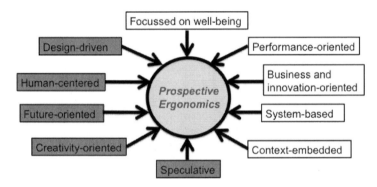

Figure 1.3. *Dimensions in white apply to general ergonomics. Dimensions highlighted in gray specifically apply to PE*

All facets of ergonomics carry elements of prospection. The concept of prospection also brings ergonomics, which mainly engages in addressing preventive and corrective human machine issues in certain contextual settings, closer to the field of design. Furthermore, with the proliferation of service, interaction and sustainable design, where innovation is usually a concern of many stakeholders, the field of ergonomics is extended to PE and design to strategic design. As shown in Figure 1.3, "design driven", "human centered", "creativity-oriented", "future-oriented" and "speculative" are typical dimensions, which have been adopted from design.

Management and Ergonomic Approaches toward Innovation and Design

2.1. History and definition of strategy

Complementary to Chapter 1, the purpose of this section is to provide a historical strategy perspective on ergonomics as certain events in the development of business strategies have a human impact which to some extent challenge the traditional view on strategy. For example, stakeholder involvement, value chains, resource-based views (RBV) [BAR 91], dynamic capabilities [TEE 97], etc., have impacted the definition of strategy[1] towards being more comprehensive and context driven. According to Nag *et al.* [NAG 07], strategic management deals with how major intended and emergent initiatives match the internal organization of companies and use of resources to enhance their performance. Moreover, developments in strategic management, where firms focus on pluralistic objectives, combined with a user experience centered view on consumerism, gave rise to the design and development of intangible-dominant commodities, such as services. Successively, service innovation [MIL 93], service design, product service system development, etc., reemphasized the importance of a systemic approach in strategizing, where deliberate planning resulted in innovation

---

1 (1) The science and art of employing the political, economic, psychological and military forces of a nation or group of nations to afford the maximum support to adopted policies in peace or war; (2) the science and art of military command exercised to meet the enemy in combat under advantageous conditions; (3) a careful plan or method; (4) the art of devising or employing plans toward a goal; (5) an adaptation or complex of adaptations (as of behavior, metabolism or structure) that serves or appears to serve an important function in achieving evolutionary success. Source: Merriam Webster, http://www.merriam-webster.com/dictionary/strategy

activities, centered around the user. This user- or human-centered innovation approach shares the same perspectives with prospective ergonomics (PE) and is characterized by a focus on well-being, an orientation toward the future and business making, and a need for contextual embeddedness.

A historical overview of strategy

Strategy as a measure to control market forces and shape competitive environments started as early as the second half of the 19th Century. However, the field of strategic management has advanced substantially in the past 40 years [EDW 10]. This advancement has been advocated by top executives of multidivisional formed corporations who first articulated the need for a formal approach to corporate strategy. Sloan [SLO 63] devised a strategy that was explicitly based on the perceived strengths and weaknesses of its competitor, Ford. In the 1930s, Chester Barnard, a top executive with AT&T, encouraged managers to think strategically by specifically considering "strategic factors", which depend on "personal or organizational" action. Strategic thinking and decision making were finally challenged and tested in World War II to allocate scarce resources across the entire economy to facilitate innovation in management science.

This implies that through rational and deliberate planning, initiating and carrying through changes in an economic environment, a company could exert some positive control over market forces [DRU 54]. This attitude toward rational planning and strategizing is a typical phenomenon associated with Taylorism and opposed by ergonomists. In the late 1950s, Andrews [AND 71] elaborated on this thinking by arguing that "every business organization, every subunit of organization and even every individual needs to clearly define their purposes or goals, which keeps them moving in a deliberately chosen direction and prevents them drifting in undesired directions". By the 1960s, discussions on business policy making were focused on matching a company's "strengths" and "weaknesses" with the "opportunities" and "threats" (or risks) it faced in the marketplace. This framework, which is referred to by the acronym SWOT, was a major step forward in explicitly propelling competitive thinking toward strategy [AND 71].

This attitude of organizations that emphasize growth and diversification and are overly "willing to gamble" their distinctive competence in pursuit of opportunity was heavily criticized by Levitt [LEV 60]. His opinion was that organizations were too much focused on delivering a product, presumably capitalizing on its distinctive competence, instead of consciously serving the customer. In other words, "the reason for a company to fail is based on the inadequacy of the product to adapt to the constantly changing consumer patterns, as well as developing marketing and product developments practices in complementary industries" [LEV 60].

However, according to Ansoff [ANS 68], a company should first ask whether a new product has a "common thread" with its existing products instead of taking unnecessary risks by investing in new products that might not meet the firm's distinctive competence. Ansoff defined the common thread as a firm's "mission" or its commitment to exploit an existing need in the market as a whole and noted that sometimes the customer is wrongly identified as the main thread of a firm's business. Therefore, to maintain its strategic focus, companies need to categorize and structure their innovation intents before determining what the main thread in its business/corporate strategy is. This can be achieved by translating the result of a SWOT analysis into a series of concrete questions to be answered in the development of strategies [POR 85].

The 1960s and early 1970s witnessed the emergence of several strategy consulting practices. The Boston Consulting Group (BCG) in particular, founded in 1963, was influential in applying quantitative research to solve business problems and enhance corporate strategy. According to BCGs founder, Bruce Henderson [HEN 84], a consultant's job was to discover "meaningful quantitative relationships" between a company and its chosen markets, which means that "good strategic action" depends primarily on logic, not on experience derived from intuition. His argument was that intuition and traditional patterns of behavior, which have been successful in the past, were too much relied upon in most firms' strategizing activities. Moreover, in growth industries acting within dynamic environments, significantly accelerating changes produce a business world where there is no place for traditional managerial habits, which renders organizations increasingly inadequate [HEN 79].

Roughly at the same time as the BCG, several other consulting firms developed their own matrices for strategic business unit and portfolio analysis at roughly the same time as BCG. For instance when GE asked McKinsey & Company to examine its corporate structure, it was discovered that 200 profit centers and 145 departments were arranged around 10 groups and that the boundaries for these units had been defined according to theories of financial control, which the McKinsey consultants judged to be inadequate. They argued that the firm should adopt a more future-oriented approach by organizing itself more along strategic lines, where strategic business units are to be more concerned with external conditions rather than internal controls through the measurement of past financial performance.

This is supported by Abernathy and Wayne's [ABE 74] views that using analytical techniques to intensively pursue a cost-minimization strategy reduces an organization's ability to make innovative changes and to respond to innovations introduced by competitors. Later on, Hayes and Abernathy [HAY 80] argued that "new principles of management, despite their sophistication and widespread usefulness, encourage (1) objective analysis rather than developing insights that come from 'hands on experience' and (2) long-term development of technological competitiveness rather than short-term cost reduction". Given this context, portfolio analysis is being criticized as a financial risk management tool that holds managers back from investing in new opportunities that require a long-term commitment of resources.

A clear case which illustrates the above situation is Henry Ford's obsession with lowering costs, which made him vulnerable to Alfred Sloan's strategy of product innovation in the automotive industry.

In 1985, Porter [POR 85] suggested to analyze cost and differentiation using a "value chain" template which dissects a firm's strategizing activities in order to understand the behavior of costs and the existing and potential sources of differentiation [GHE 02]. He emphasized the importance of regrouping functions into discrete activities that support the production, marketing, delivery and development of products as competitive advantage cannot be achieved by looking at a firm as a whole. Each of these discrete activities can contribute to a firm's relative cost position and create a basis for differentiation by emphasizing their relationships and how these activities connect to the value chain. In other words, competitive advantage is created from the many interactions and dealings a firm performs within its business ecosystem. Differentiation as well as collaboration with stakeholders can contribute to a firm's relative cost position and create a basis for differentiation.

In the late 1980s and early 1990s, authorities in the field of strategic management started to confront the issues of "dynamism" when it concerns creating and sustaining competitive advantage. According to Stalk [STA 88], strategy can never be constant. For organizations to be at the cutting edge, it is and always will be a moving target, where fast response and at the cutting variety should be aimed for. Organizations without these ambitions are mainly competing on price.

In the same period, the RBV, an old idea of looking at the existing resources of an organization, has been revisited. Defined by Wernerfelt [WER 84], it is a traditional concept of strategy which emphasizes the availability of resources (strengths and weaknesses) within a firm, whereas most of our formal economic tools operate on the product market side. In support of the RBV, other resource-based theorists seek to distinguish their perspective on sustained superior performance and product market positioning from that of industrial organization economics by underlining the innate inimitability of scarce, valuable resources for a variety of reasons: the ability to acquire a particular resource may be dependent on unique, historical circumstances that competitors cannot recreate; the link between the resources possessed by a firm and its sustained competitive advantage may be causally ambiguous or poorly understood; or the resource responsible for the advantage may be socially complex and therefore "beyond the ability of firms to systematically manage and influence" (e.g., corporate culture) [BAR 91]. On a critical note, resource-based theorists have therefore perceived firms as stuck with a few key resources which they must deploy across product markets in ways that maximize total profits rather than profits in individual markets. This means that instead of focusing on products, organizations should nurture underlying core competencies and resources in a way to unbound innovation and in the long run spawn unanticipated new products" [PRA 90].

In the 1990s, a number of strategy scholars extended the resource-based view by explaining how firm-specific dynamic capabilities perform activities better and are redeployed over long periods of time. The dynamic-capabilities view of the firm differs from the RBV because capabilities are to be developed and nurtured rather than taken for granted, which has been pioneered and described more extensively by Teece et al. [TEE 97].

In summary, the transition from the 20th to 21st Century can be characterized by firms' sustainable, long-term profit making ambitions, supported by a dynamic and RBV view on how to allocate and grow internal resources as well as how to build and nurture external networks.

2.2. Management and design frameworks supporting PE

The purpose of discussing a selection of theoretical frameworks in this chapter is to anchor PE within the broader context of ergonomics and strategic management, as well as to explore synergies between this new field of ergonomics and strategic design. Figure 2.1 depicts the relationship between management, design and ergonomic topics, centered around PE.

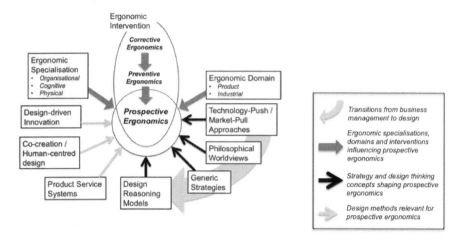

Figure 2.1. *Selected theoretical frameworks and methods to conceptualize prospective ergonomics*

To form the foundation for this thesis, selected theoretical frameworks and methods from the fields of strategic management, product planning, strategic/system design and design reasoning feed into the main theme "prospective ergonomics". These frameworks, which will be elaborated more in the following sections, are as follows:

- technology push–market pull;

- worldviews and design reasoning modes;

- generic business strategies;

- product service systems (PSS);

- co-creation and human-centered design;

- design-driven innovation.

2.2.1. *Technology push versus market pull*

As the global environment is becoming increasingly competitive and dynamic, organizations and businesses are continuously challenged to look for the most efficient ways to maximize their innovation and management efforts using new models, methods and paradigms, which efficiently serve existing and new markets with new and/or modified products as well as services [CHR 00]. Damanpour [DAM 91] has extended the definition of innovation beyond the creation and market introduction of new products or services by claiming that it can also be a new technology or structure to improve production and administrative systems, or a new plan or program to facilitate collaboration among stakeholders. This implies that in the pursuit of radical innovation, global trends need to be taken into account in the planning of future products, services and contexts [FIN 09]. Hereby, innovation push and pull models are helpful to characterize drivers for innovation. Traditionally, push-innovation referred to knowledge- or technology-driven innovation. Although technology push has been considered as a first and important generation of innovation strategy [ROU 91], design-driven innovation, originating from an internal knowledge-building within companies and among stakeholders and interpreters, has recently been advocated as most relevant in discovering hidden needs [VER 08, RAM 11].

Simplistically, managers of technological enterprises can be segmented in two camps: those who believe that markets direct their course of action and those who proclaim that their technology will develop a following [SUK 11]. Those who need to define a market beforehand are marketing managers while engineers and technologists adopt a more constructive approach. The range of recent innovations such as polyester tires, ceramic engines, superconductivity and personal computers challenge marketers and engineers to adopt both a positivist as well as constructivist approach. Can a marketing manager make a list of all of the inventions which he has never heard of? Similarly, can a technologist predict all applications (i.e. needs) for nylon or integrated circuits?

Given this context, firms, both large and small, require both technology-push and market-pull approaches in order to be continuously innovative and profitable.

A matrix, juxtaposing rationalist-historicist and empirical-idealistic dimensions, illustrates the different relationships of technology-push and market-pull approaches with respect to four different types of innovation:

user-driven, market-driven, design-driven and technology-driven[2] (Figure 2.2) [LIE 12].

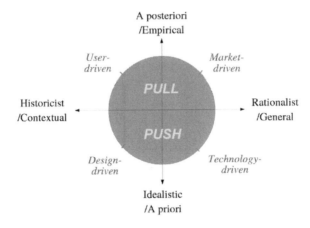

Figure 2.2. *Rationalist-historicist and empirical-idealistic dimensions contextualized and positioned according to different technology-push and market-pull approaches (adopted from [MØR 11, p. 214]*

A historicist view on innovation shows a more constructivist conception of the process as a whole, characterized by an iterative cycle of concept development and testing of solutions. A rational view perceives knowledge to be applied independently of a specific setting, at least to a certain degree. An empirical/*a posteriori* perspective represents a "pull" approach, whether market- or user-driven. This means that "data" are a prerequisite for a firm to initiate innovation. Supporters of the idealistic/*a priori* perspective are convinced that radical innovation should come from either a technology or design "push" approach. They are skeptical that breakthrough innovations can be systematically and empirically analyzed only through data.

However, technological developments and market structures are influential in how the product, system or service is being divided into

---

2 User-driven innovation means that a firm involves its users directly in the product creation process. Market-driven innovation is an innovation approach determined or responsive to market forces. Technology-driven innovation is an approach that pushes for development of new goods or services based on a firm's technical abilities instead of proven demand. Design-driven innovation is an approach on how to innovate new products and services which give meaning.

interconnecting entities. As an example, Ansoff's perspective on innovation strategy can be seen as an essential tool for directing market and technological research [ANS 80], whereas Mintzberg's strategy model suits a context-based user or design-driven innovation process better [MIN 87]. Both perspectives are considered as equivalent to the push and pull models of innovation. The description is polarized in order to contrast the different models of innovation and to facilitate the positioning of different ergonomic interventions and specializations.

In user-centered innovation, product development activities start from a deep analysis of user needs, where researchers immerse themselves in fieldwork by observing customers and their environments to acquire a detailed understanding of customer's lifestyles and cultures as a foundation for better discerning their needs and problems [BEL 04]. Latest developments in innovation activities involving users have questioned the creative effectiveness of user-centered design methods from a participatory design (PD) and generative design research perspective, characterized by co-creation methods [SAN 08]. PD is an approach to assess, design and develop technological and organizational systems, whereby active involvement of potential or current end-users as well as other stakeholders is encouraged in design and decision-making processes.

Similar to technology-driven innovation, design-driven innovation has largely remained unexplored. Moreover, unlike user-centered processes, it is less based on using formal roles, processes and methods, such as ethnographic research. Design-driven innovation may be perceived as a manifestation of a reconstructionist [MAU 05] or social constructionist view of the market [PRA 00], where the market is not "given" *a priori* but is the social construct of interactions between consumers and firms Hereby, stakeholders need to understand the radically new language and message, to find new connections and meanings to their sociocultural context and to explore new symbolic values and patterns of interaction with the product, which are not only livable and sustainable but also fun and culturally inspiring [ESS 11].

In other words, sociocultural regimes are profoundly solicited by radical innovations, similar to the way fundamental changes in technological regimes are devised by radical technological innovations [GEE 04].

2.2.2. *Philosophical worldviews*

Although philosophical worldviews remain most often largely hidden in the design world, they still influence the practice of design and need to be identified. As explained by Creswell [CRE 09] and Lincoln and Guba [LIN 85], a worldview can be defined as "a compilation of fundamental beliefs that guide action" and is similar to a paradigm or epistemology.

The types of philosophical worldviews held by individual designers will often have great impact on their approaches to design theories and indirectly on the concrete methods and techniques they use. Four different worldviews are briefly presented in Figure 2.3 [LIE 14], based on the work of Creswell [CRE 09] on research design (and the use of qualitative, quantitative or mixed research methods).

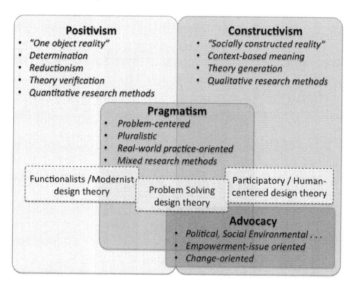

Figure 2.3. *Overview of presented worldviews and design theories [LIE 14]*

It should be noted that the presented worldviews may take various forms and may use principles that are comparable and complementary from one another. They are not considered as rigid and separate but rather may overlap each other to varying degrees. For the alignment of selected worldviews with ergonomic interventions, positivism and constructivism in their most literal form have been presented here as contradictive and irreconcilable (see Figure 2.3, [LIN 85]). However, one should note that according to "constructivist realism", worlds are multilayered with many levels of interacting structures on-going simultaneously [CUP 01]. This is reinforced by the on-going trend toward the reconciliation of positivism and constructivism, which can be achieved by eliminating the arbitrary boundaries and assumptions concerning truth and apprehension. For instance, postpositivism offers a vision that is more nuanced and better suited for the study of design science; it recognizes that knowledge is conjectural and absolute truth can never be found when studying humans [PHI 00]. Constructivism is affiliated with postmodernism, whereby truth is perceived to be grounded in everyday life and social relations, and knowledge is created from different sources and experiences. It is significantly different from postpositivism because we are constrained by our own perception and as such cannot access reality and that which we consider to be reality is constructed. In other words, the observer and the observed cannot be separated; reality is co-constructed by individuals in a social context, where beliefs change over time [LIN 85].

Although pragmatism makes use of elements from both postpositivism and constructivism, it remains a worldview on its own and is not committed to one system of philosophy and reality [CRE 09]. Great emphasis is placed on focusing on a problem and the use of pluralistic approaches to derive knowledge about the problem. As researchers have the freedom to choose methods, techniques and procedures for research, stands are not taken on the debate of reality as objective or subjective but on how they best meet their needs and purpose [CRE 09, ROR 90].

Advocacy criticizes the fact that constructivism does not go far enough in advocating for marginalized people [CRE 09]. With respect to stakeholder involvement in a human-centered design context, individuals should be included in prospective ergonomic research and design in order not to be further marginalized or limited in self determination and self-development.

The relationship between the different worldviews and PE can be argued from a "human" interest perspective. Understanding present and designing future contexts with respect to well-being as well as economic sustainability are most likely to be facilitated by adopting a constructivist, advocacy and partly pragmatic worldview in addition to positivistic ways of "doing things":

– the constructivist worldview contextualizes the fact that human activities are unpredictable and subject to external influences; social, economic and political, as well as internal ambitions, which can sometimes be erratic, illogical, idealistic, etc. In line with PE and strategic design, designers seek to capture the complexity of views instead of narrowing them to a few categories of ideas. Hereby, subjective meanings are socially and historically influenced, and research focuses on the contexts and interactions among individuals, which is different from postpositivist research where interpretation of observations is influenced by the background of the researcher;

– the pragmatic worldview acknowledges that humans need systems and systematic planning but since they do not have an infinite knowledge framework, planning happens within predetermined contexts. These predetermined contexts are more supportive of a corrective or preventive way of solving ergonomic design problems, assuming that an ideology or proposition is true as long as it works satisfactorily;

– the advocacy worldview connects well with PE, as it lays the foundation for developing persuasive concepts and socially responsible solutions to promote future well-being for people.

To summarize this section, the dual objective of PE, which is, on the one hand, to promote well-being and, on the other hand, facilitate innovation, requires designers and ergonomists to plan the development of products and services, while taking into consideration contextual constraints, possibilities and responsibilities. With respect to worldview adoption, these designers and ergonomists need to embrace all the four worldviews, because PE resides in systemic ways of strategizing (see section 2.3), where processes are deliberate and targeted outcomes are plural.

Section 2.2.3 maps out four generic strategies to provide a clearer picture why a systemic generic strategy is very much related to PE with respect to thought, process and ambition.

2.2.3. *Four perspectives on strategy*

The motivation behind a company's vision and choice of strategy is usually encapsulated in various theories of action in order to achieve competitive advantage [WHI 01]. To provide decision makers with fundamentally different ways of thinking about strategy in a wide range of situations, four perspectives on strategy were created and mapped according to process and outcome (see Figure 2.4). These perspectives, which are classical, evolutionary, processual, and systemic, have their roots in "Mintzberg's 10 Schools of Thought about Strategy Formation" [MIN 85].

As a precursor to Whittington's generic strategy perspectives, these schools were compared and positioned on a bipolar spectrum according to planned and emergent strategies [MIN 89].

When addressing the "outcomes" axis, the "plural" dimension should be interpreted from a more nuanced perspective, considering both the short and the long term, as well as diverse ambitions of internal and external stakeholders, in contrast to the focused profit-maximizing aims of the organization leadership. The "processes" axis illustrates a spectrum between deliberate and emergent ways of planning.

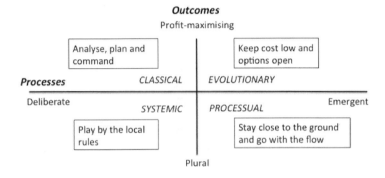

Figure 2.4. *Overview of generic strategy perspectives [WHI 01]*

In the classical approach, profit-maximizing is the highest goal of business and rational planning. This classical theory claims that if returns-on-investments are not satisfactory in the long run, the deficiency of the business venture should be corrected or abandoned [SLO 63]. Key features of the classical approach are the attachment to rational analysis, the separation between planning and execution, and the commitment to profit maximization [ANS 68, SLO 63].

Evolutionary approaches are characterized by an on-going struggle for survival through reactive decision making. In the search for profit maximization, natural selection will determine who are the best performers and the ones that survive [EIN 81].

In contrast to classical and evolutionary approaches, processual methods do not aim for profit-maximization ambitions, but strive to work with what reality offers. Practically, this means that firms are not always united. Instead, individuals with different interests, acting in an environment of confusion and mess, determine the course of action. Through a process of internal bargaining within the organization, members set goals among themselves, which are acceptable to all.

In a systemic approach, the organization is not made up simply of individuals acting purely in economic transactions but of individuals embedded in a network of densely interwoven social relations that may involve their family, state, professional and educational backgrounds, even their culture, religion and ethnicity [WHI 01].

2.3. Aligning generic strategies with innovation approaches through worldview perspectives

Using different worldview perspectives, alignments can be established between Whittington's generic strategy perspectives and the technology-push/market-pull innovation approaches, as shown in Figure 2.5. Although these alignments can be perceived to be rather simplistic, it explains the most dominant relationships between typical worldviews, strategy perspectives and innovation approaches. In each of the following four sections, the connection between (technology-push/market-pull) innovation approaches and generic strategy perspectives will be elaborated through a worldview transfer.

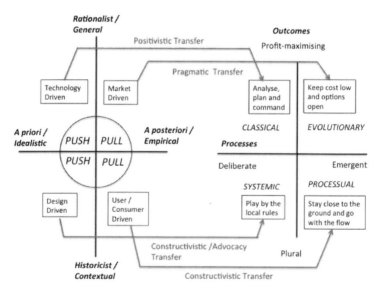

Figure 2.5. *Alignment of innovation approaches with generic strategies through a worldview perspective*

2.3.1. *A technology-driven innovation approach based on a generic classical strategy*

Besides sharing positivistic characteristics of "doing things in a top-down, structured and directive manner" between technology-driven marketing and classical strategy approaches, "good business model" design and implementation, coupled with careful strategic analysis, are necessary for technological innovation to succeed commercially [TEE 10, p. 184]. This statement implies that every new technology-driven product development effort should be coupled with the development of a planned business strategy, which defines its "go to market" and when and how to "capture optimal economic value strategies". Based on a continuous spectrum, the following concrete examples show possible planned strategies which a company can adopt:

– at one end of the scale, an integrated business model is being applied where an innovating firm takes responsibility for the entire value chain from A to Z including design, manufacturing and distribution by grouping innovation and product design activities together;

– the other extreme case is the outsourced (pure licensing) business approach, which has been adopted by several companies;

– in between there are hybrid approaches involving a mixture of the two approaches (e.g. outsource manufacturing, provide company-owned sales and support). Hybrid approaches are the most common but they also require strong selection and organization skills on the part of management [TEE 07].

2.3.2. *A design-driven innovation approach based on a generic systemic strategy*

In the broader context of creativity, design is the engine to manage complex human needs. Designers and their business partners have a unique obligation and opportunity to build an environment where actors, consumers, users and other stakeholders, are members of a larger interdependent community rooted deeply in densely interwoven social systems. Hereby, these actors should not be seen as decision makers, who are simply detached calculative individuals, interacting in a purely transactional manner in an economic sense [GRA 85]. To be more specific, people's economic behavior is embedded in a network of social relations involving their families, state, their educational and professional backgrounds, religion and ethnicity [SWE 87, WHI 92]. This systemic view on strategizing aligns well with the concept of "design-driven" innovation and "technology-driven" innovation, which have earlier been explained in section 2.2.1.

Particularly in "design-driven" innovation, deliberate attempts to create radical change through meaning-making in the design of products and services have been promoted by Norman and Verganti [NOR 14] through their framework on technology–push innovation, market–pull innovation, meaning-driven innovation and technology epiphanies. This framework will be elaborated upon in section 2.8.5, upon contextualization with ergonomic domains, specializations and interventions.

The alignment between a design-driven market approach and a systemic way of strategizing is commonly represented by its context dependency. People in organizations strategize and consumers make sense of a product or service according to their psychological profile and the cultural and social context in which they are immersed. Interpretations of meanings are constructed and reconstructed in an ongoing co-creation process through continuous interactions among firms, designers, users and several stakeholders, both inside and outside a corporation [BRO 91, TSO 96]. The innovation of meaning, therefore, could be linked to a social constructivist [BUR 10, LAN 95] or even reconstructivist [CHA 05] approach, where the interaction of objects and subjects mutually "shapes" or "constructs" representations of reality in a continuous process. The constructivist transfer, which is hermeneutic in nature, suggests that innovation is the act of envisioning new meanings. It is not simply about generating ideas and solutions but about strategically creating a whole new vision. Hereby, the act of interpretation is based on a deliberate creation of new interpretations that do not yet exist by involving a broader range of interpreters and experts.

2.3.3. *A user-driven innovation approach based on a generic processual strategy*

The connectivity between a user/consumer-driven perspective toward innovation and how this is being facilitated by a processual strategy is dependent on how organizations transform themselves to become more consumer oriented. This transformation can take place when these organizations are willing to introduce novel tools, instruments and procedures to systematically and continuously integrate users into their core business processes. Enabling users to interact with each other in real time and reflectively exchange and discuss ideas or to provide feedback and support is a vital prerequisite for fostering creativity during ideation processes [HIE 11]. The link with the processual characteristics of strategizing is established by rejecting the existence of the rational man, as well as perfect functioning competitive markets [CYE 63]. Acknowledging the limits of human cognition, people within organizations and therefore organizations are rationally bounded. Similarly, users, who are involved in co-creating products, services and businesses, are unable to consider more than a handful factors at one time. Biased in their interpretation of data and limited in communicating all their needs, designers and ergonomists are inclined to adopt a reactive and reflective practice approach toward creativity and problem solving. To summarize this section, doing things in an evolving manner centered on people is a typical trait of user-centric strategizing when objectives are plural and stakeholders accept and work with the world as it is.

2.3.4. A market-driven innovation approach based on a generic evolutionary strategy

Supporters of the evolutionary perspective on strategizing are less confident that top managers and decision makers are fully capable of planning and acting rationally. By adopting a postpositivistic and pragmatic worldview, they believe that markets dictate how profit maximization can be achieved. By association with the "law of the jungle", only the best performers will survive. Therefore, managers need not be rational optimizers because "evolution is nature's cost benefit analysis". However, this does not mean that companies need to take an *ad hoc* approach toward innovation [CLA 11]. They need to continuously connect with increasingly complex consumer demands as well as exploit the technological capabilities they possess, or acquire new ones. The differences with the other innovation and generic strategy alignments, such as the "user driven – processual" alignment, are that in this market-driven innovation approach consumer behaviors are essential but the consumer/user him or herself is not expected to be involved in creativity or co-creation activities. In other words, the consumer is seen as a passive rather than an active participator. From the offering point of view and based on the (dynamic) capabilities of the companies, the evolutionary way of strategizing is to maximize profit by betting on different incremental innovation projects and initiatives, rather than carefully planning a single penetration strategy for achieving "radical" innovation. The reason why certain companies choose to strategize in an opportunistic manner is based on their belief that it is becoming more difficult to predict the future because of globalization trends, changing economic, social and political climates, and increasingly complex consumer demands. Furthermore, companies are being increasingly subjected to dynamic internal and contextual demands, which makes it extra challenging for decision makers to plan future products and services.

2.4. Toward integrated thinking in PE: relating C-K design theory, generic strategies and design reasoning models

In this section, C-K design theory, generic strategies and models of design reasoning will be discussed within the context of management and design thinking to develop the argument that PE is founded upon "integrated thinking". In developing this argument, it is necessary to juxtapose C-K theory with generic strategies, on the one hand, and C-K theory with models of design reasoning, on the other hand. Juxtapositioning leads to the following:

– in concurrence with Hatchuel's work, strategic management is challenged to become more pluralistic by aiming to be inclusive, human centered and empathic in seeking co-created solutions to problems [HAT 10, p. 11]. Hereby, design thinking around business making may facilitate pluralistic ambitions, as it builds on principles of integrative thinking;

– with respect to different modes of design reasoning and philosophical worldviews, abductive logic that lies between "the past-data-driven world of analytical thinking and the knowing-without-reasoning world of intuitive thinking forms the basis for "integrated thinking" [MAR 09, p. 26];

– the meaning of "integrated thinking" for PE is that positivist and constructive worldviews, as well as problem solving/pragmatic versus reflective/hermeneutic ways of reasoning may alternate in the search for future innovative products and services. In other words, this dualistic way of reasoning based upon supposedly contradictory worldviews and immersed in a systemic generic strategy, bounded by rationality, describes the main characteristics of PE.

Referring to the qualities of C-K design theory with respect to the above three points, I believe it is most appropriate to elaborate on C-K design theory [HAT 03] to justify the interconnectivities among worldviews, generic strategies and models of "design" reasoning [LIE 12].

2.4.1. *C-K design theory*

Hatchuel and Weil [HAT 03] introduced concept–knowledge theory (or C–K theory), which has gained significant academic and industrial interest over the past 10 years. The theory is based upon the understanding that concepts are generated from existing knowledge, as well as that knowledge is explored through concepts [HAT 10]. Recently, features of this theory have been recognized as being unique for describing creative reasoning and processes in engineering design, highlighting the fact that one of the most noticeable features of C–K theory is founded on the notion of a creative concept [ULL 12]. Hereby, two discourses of strategy as design have been introduced [HAT 10, p. 12]: "strategy as analysis and implementation" and "strategy as innovation". Similar work in the field of architecture has been undertaken by Bamford [BAM 02], where analysis/synthesis has been rejected in favor of conjecture/analysis.

A key issue in C–K theory is how designers, managers and other stakeholders evaluate dependencies between what is yet-to-exist (a set of variants for a seed project with innovative elements) and what is known (and hence, what can be used as a resource for the design process). The claim of the theory is that this conceptual reasoning process is about defining essential characteristics of design, which is fundamentally different from processes prevalent in formal sciences (i.e. deductive or inductive processes) [AGO 13]. In other words, to offer a perspective where creative thinking and innovation are to be included within the core of design theory is to provide a logical and precise definition of design [HAT 03, pp. 1–2].

More concretely, design can be perceived as a coexpansion activity from two spaces: spaces of concepts (C) and spaces of knowledge (K). The expansion is transitional and can be noted as C⇒K and K⇒ C. With reference to the "design square", knowledge can be expanded internally at a concept level through inclusion or partition as well as at a knowledge level through deduction and experimentation. Transformations from K⇒C, which are "disjunctions", are typical characteristics of a positivistic problem solving process in design. Reversely, a transformation from C⇒K, which is a conjunction, can be perceived as a constructivist move toward the expansion of the knowledge space. At this point, it is too early to make clear connections and alignments between C–K theories and generic strategies. However, in terms of worldview positioning, the K⇒K and K⇒C transformations are typically positivistic and pragmatic movements, whereas C⇒C and C⇒K movements are driven by constructivism and advocacy. For example, the emergence of crazy ideas may have found their roots in spontaneous and *ad hoc* inspirations or suppressed beliefs concerning social, political, economical, ethical, etc., issues.

As anticipated in section 2.5, the contribution of C–K theory to PE is relevant because it involves different worldviews and models of design reasoning. For example, K⇒C⇒K movements are driven by positivism and pragmatism followed by constructivism and advocacy.

2.4.2. *Six models of design reasoning*

The adoption of Lie's categorization is based upon how the authors view the current discourse, which demarcates theoretical traditions with respect to models of design reasoning. Lie's extensive literature review has led to a systematic framework [LIE 12, p. 68], which illustrates the current dispute between positivistic/deliberate design approaches on the one hand and the more plural, reflected and embedded design approaches on the other. The way Lie has managed to make the dispute explicit will be relevant for design practitioners and researchers for taking stands in the "strategic" design of new products. The six models of design reasoning are "problem solving", "hermeneutic", "reflective practice", "participatory", "social" and "normative".

In this section, models of design reasoning and worldviews will be discussed and aligned with a generic strategy framework [WHI 01]. This framework shows existing relations and conjectures among these theories (see Figure 2.6) which are necessary to justify the close relationship between design thinking and business strategizing. Furthermore, this integrated framework argues that service design and the design of PSS are typical fields which meet the characteristics of a pluralistic way of strategizing. Complementary to this pluralistic way of strategizing, human-centered management and design methods are being advocated to promote the design of products and services.

Although processes and outcomes are different for strategizing and designing, the understanding of similarities among different generic strategies, worldviews and models of design reasoning will be invaluable for ergonomists, designers and business managers to create better products, systems and services. This understanding will lead to an appreciation that strategic perspectives and design reasoning modes are somehow similar in nature in the exploration of innovation attitudes. Furthermore, this alignment will provide a better understanding on how to position ergonomic domains, interventions and specializations relative to strategic management, strategic design and industrial design theories. The following sections will elaborate more on these similarities.

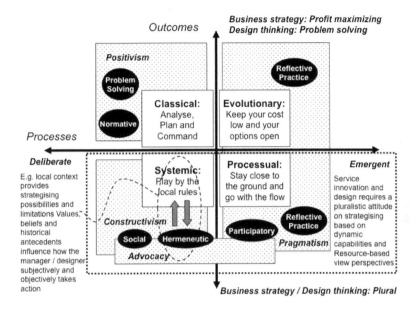

Figure 2.6. *Extension of generic strategies to models of design reasoning based upon philosophical worldviews ([LIE 14], adapted from [WHI 01, Figure 2.1, p. 10])*

A positivist worldview underpins the classical strategy approach, where profit making is planned and commanded. This is in line with a focused and structured problem-solving approach, where a systematic design process [ROO 95] defines the solution space. The normative reasoning model is exemplified by how a strict and concrete program of requirements complements this problem-solving approach. Typically, PMT-matrices [ANS 68] and style/technology maps [CAG 02] are examples of methods and tools which support a planned and structured approach toward innovation and design.

The evolutionary and processual strategic approaches are built upon a pragmatic worldview. Lacking a debate as to whether reality is objective or subjective, the emergent and in some cases opportunistic characteristics of these strategies determine how organizations behave to achieve their profit-making targets or goals. For instance, within corrective ergonomics, an evolutionary business strategy, complemented by a reflective way of designing, would suffice to incrementally improve ergonomic functionality of existing products.

Similarly, there are design-reasoning attitudes which can be aligned with these emergent approaches. The reflective practice addresses design issues from a constructivist, though pragmatic, perspective by engaging in conjectural conversations with the situation [SCH 95]. The participatory element, where different stakeholders are actively or passively involved in the design process, bringing along their personal interests, is a real-life and pragmatic phenomenon, which aligns well with an emergent strategy driven by pluralistic objectives but which may not always lead to profit-maximizing or optimal, economical design solutions. To address such a complex situation, which emphasizes well-being, PE may facilitate the discovery of hidden needs and anticipate future solutions.

The systemic strategy is socially constructed and therefore the reality is coconstructed by different stakeholders and individuals in a social context [LIN 85]. Although processes are planned and deliberate, multiple objectives exist because of the complexity of multiple views, which are socially, historically, culturally and contextually embedded in respective communities of practice. Considering a community of design practitioners, the use of selected methods and tools, combined with personal experience and subjectivity, occupies a central place in the design process, which is based on hermeneutic and social reasoning. From PE and strategic design perspectives, the designer attempts to anticipate human needs and activities so as to create new artifacts and services that will be useful and provide a positive user experience [ROB 09]. Reiterating the importance of systemic embeddedness, contexts, values and functions should be considered here as a key element in getting any collaborative process going that involves different stakeholders.

2.5. A PSS perspective

As technological products continue to converge and become increasingly more important in consumer's daily lives, service expectations continue to rise. This trend instigated a shift from production to utilization, from product to process, and from transaction to relationship [VAR 08], demanding a PSS thinking perspective toward ergonomics.

Complementary to this PSS view on ergonomics, Dul *et al.* [DUL 12] identified that the potential of human factors (HF) is underexploited because stakeholders in design and management of organizations are mainly focused on performance outcome. Even though there is some recognition among design and engineering practitioners and researchers about the potential benefits in applying HF in design, it is not sufficient [BAN 02]. The lack of HF being applied in design is also explained by Hollnagel and Woods [HOL 05]. Traditional ergonomics never questioned the validity of the human–machine distinction and therefore encountered problems in developing a systems view comprising stakeholder interactions in context.

As such, Norros [NOR 14] perceived a pressing need for conceptual innovation. This means that within a systems frame of reference, HF is to be design-driven as well as focused on two closely related outcomes: "performance" and "well-being" [DUL 12, p. 1].

In this context, the design of a system should be comprehended as a process of continuous redesign, where actors are involved in reconstructing and modifying the system in the course of their daily activities. Based upon the resource-based view and dynamic capabilities theories [TEE 97], the basis of learning processes are derived from handling the many deviations from "the normal" procedure assumed by the designers [WEI 99]. This implies that over time system actors inevitably also play the role of system redesigners.

Based upon consumer-centric and plural intraorganizational perspectives [MIC 08], companies are challenged to conceptualize PSS that are perceived as valuable by all, extending the service-dominant logic to a larger, complex network of collaborating actors [VAR 08]. With respect to the deliberate modes of business strategizing, trends influencing PSS will be elaborated in this separate chapter to address the importance of a balanced approach in achieving performance and well-being within the context of strategic design and PE. The emergence of these trends can be attributed to the increasing complexities of technology and customer demands, driven by globalization. A systems approach, which concerns all stages of planning, designing, implementation, evaluation, maintenance and redesigning [JAP 06], matches with the ergonomic intervention on the product development process of Nelson *et al.* [NEL 12] (see Figure 1.2). Centered on design, these stages are not necessarily sequential; they are recursive, interdependent and dynamic. Decisions at one stage may influence or be influenced by decisions at other stages. This means that systems change because of the fluidity of the human or the environmental part of the system or both. However, ergonomics has the potential to contribute to the design of future systems by contributing fundamental characteristics through explicit design approaches, methods and tools as well as implicit modes of interaction in the search for innovative product and service design solutions in the fuzzy–front end stages of the design process.

In order to plan an effective innovation strategy for the future, key global developments and trends, as well as their significance for ergonomics, need to be identified through analyses and assessments resulting in recommendations and actions [HEN 91, JAP 06]. Without being complete, important issues that impact ergonomics are "global change of work systems", "cultural diversity", "aging", "information communication and technonology (ICT)", "enhanced competitiveness and the need for innovation" and "sustainability and corporate social responsibility" (CSR). These issues will be discussed in the following sections with respect to PE and strategic design.

2.5.1. *Impact of global economic changes on work systems*

Over the past decade, significant shifts in the types of work that occur in different regions of the world have been motivated by global changes in the economic landscape. These changes have taken place in both economically advanced nations and economically developing nations. Historically, economically advanced nations have been mass-producing goods. However, due to global market forces and the intensification of supply chains, these nations increasingly outsourced manufacturing and service functions to economically developing countries over the past two decades [DUL 12]. The emphasis in economically advanced nations has then shifted from a production to a service economy (including healthcare services), resulting in a greater focus on both the design of work systems for service production, as well as on the design of non-work systems such as services for customers and human–computer interactions [DRU 08, HED 08].

At the same time, developing countries have enlarged their economic activities through low-cost manufacturing of goods, as well as simultaneously experiencing an increase in low-wage service sector jobs (e.g. call centers, banking) [CAP 08].

Furthermore, the continuing trend of mechanization and automation of work systems, resulting in increased capabilities of technology, not only impacts the manufacturing but also service industry [SCH 09]. These phenomena changed attitudes and perceptions among stakeholders who are providing and receiving services whether or not they are complemented by products.

2.5.2. *HF and cultural diversity*

In many economically developed and developing countries, the understanding of the human element requires knowledge of complex, social and cultural environments. This can be attributed to global change, which proved to be instrumental in increasing interdependencies among economies, industries and companies worldwide. Consequently, production and distribution systems are internationally structured by implementing culturally diverse workforces to facilitate that products and services are consumed by increasingly diverse groups of customers in markets around the world [DUL 12]. As a result, (work) environments and product–consumer systems that were properly designed for one society may not be appropriate for other societies because of different cultural backgrounds, different characteristics and aspirations.

This trend of cultural diversity positions ergonomics within a systemic management strategy by contributing to the cross-cultural design of production, distribution systems as well as products and services that fit the diversity of users and other stakeholders [MOR 00, JAP 06]. In cross-cultural design, it is generally agreed upon that people from different cultures have different capabilities and aspirations, which affect the design of the product–service systems in which they take part.

2.5.3. *Demographic change*

A demographic change is generally experienced in most developed parts of the world, brought about by a combination of longer life expectancy, declining fertility and the progression through life of a large "baby boom" generation [DUL 12]. In the United States and Europe, the proportion of older people in the workforce is increasing more than in other continents, whereas in India, Asia and especially Southeast Asia, the retirement age of office and industrial workers has recently been raised. As a result, a large group of senior workers has become part of work and product/service environments that were initially designed and more suited for a younger group of people. Implications are that work systems comprising equipment, furniture, IT devices, services, etc., need to be reevaluated and targeted to an older population and adapted to their characteristics, without stigmatizing them. Hereby, ergonomists need to take into account age-related changes in physical, cognitive, visual and other capabilities, and different aspirations [JAP 06].

Prospectively, there is room for developing more versatile systems that are better matched to a wide range of groups. As such, a universal design approach does not only apply to people of different age groups but also to people with disabilities [BUC 11].

2.5.4. *Influence of ICT in shaping future living*

According to Karwowski [KAR 06], several ICT-related challenges impact the manner in which work and activities of daily living are performed. For instance, rapid and continuous developments in computer science, telecommunication and media technology have increased and accelerated information transfer through new interactive activities such as social media and gaming. As a result, people's social and working lives have become more and more dependent on ICT and virtual networks. In addition, product quality is valued beyond usability by emphasizing emotional design and pleasurable interactions.

ICT developments have brought about many changes in work organization and organizational design. For example, in the manufacturing sector, increasingly, organizational networks and supply chains are relying on virtual arrangements to communicate and share information. Another example resides in healthcare, where different healthcare organizations share information about patients.

Within the context of ICT, ergonomic specialists contribute to the design of virtual sociotechnical systems to engage diverse people who are geographically dispersed. They facilitate the use of information and communication technologies among these people to perform their work remotely and share information across organizational boundaries [WOO 00, GIB 06]. However, one of the many challenges is how to design natural user interfaces and influence the design of virtual sociotechnical systems in human–computer interactions, which can enhance trust and collaboration when team members work remotely and communicate via technology [PAT 12].

2.5.5. *The need for innovation to enhance competitiveness*

Globalization has forced companies to develop new business strategies and alliances to become more competitive. Additionally, it has also pressured companies to increase innovation and invention of new products and services, as well as new ways of producing these. To be successful in the market and to gain commercial advantage, these products and services must be of high quality and serve beyond technical functionality, for example by adding value in terms of positive emotional user experiences. Complementarily, production processes need to be more efficient and flexible and must guarantee short product delivery times, often resulting in intensification of work.

In the process of renewing business strategies and product/service innovation, ergonomics enhances and fosters employee creativity [DUL 11, DUL 09] as well as facilitates in developing new products and services with unique usability and experience qualities. It can also assist a company to innovate processes and operations by providing new efficient and effective ways of producing these products and services [BRO 97, BRU 00].

2.5.6. *Sustainability and CSR*

Sustainability, which deals with the needs of the present without compromising those of future generations, not only emphasizes natural and physical resources ("planet"), but also human and social resources ("people") in combination with economic sustainability ("profit") [DEL 10, PFE 10]. Rather than purely focusing on financial performance, it claims that companies act to fulfill a broader range of pluralistic objectives. For example, being corporately and socially responsible, companies take up the challenge to meet the minimum legal expectations regarding "planet" and "people". A company's image with respect to CSR may be damaged by poor or minimum health and safety standards, which would be a direct threat to the continuity of the business. Given this challenge, ergonomics can support sustainability and CSR activities within organizations by adopting a forward-looking approach in developing programs that combine the people and profit dimension through the optimization of both performance and well-being [PFE 10, ZIN 05].

In conclusion, global developments, which have been discussed in sections 2.6.1–2.6.6, argue for the need for a new type of ergonomics, namely PE, which focuses on managing and solving complex societal issues. Besides being systems oriented, this type of ergonomics should also be forward looking in time, because these developments continue to have future implications. Moreover, by taking a proactive role in shaping future living and working environments, PE requires taking responsibility for cross-disciplinary work [NOR 14]. For example, the intervention of PE in strategic design provides ample opportunities for collaborating with the design research as well as design community, which may lead to a richer collection of concepts for anticipating future living and working conditions.

3

Ergonomic Interventions
on Management Frameworks

In this chapter, selected theoretical frameworks and methods from business strategizing, innovation and design will be discussed and aligned with different ergonomic domains, interventions and specializations. Prior to this alignment, comparisons were made among ergonomic interventions, strategic design and management perspectives.

The alignment is built upon a main frame, where rationalist–historicist and empirical–idealistic dimensions are contextualized according to different technology-push and market-pull approaches. Moreover, the connectivity among generic strategies, worldviews and models of design reasoning is positioned according to a framework of deliberate versus emergent processes and singular versus plural outcomes. To mark the human factor in the strategy and management frameworks, different ergonomic interventions and specializations will be positioned according to strategic perspectives and other positioning maps.

3.1. A comparison of ergonomic interventions with strategic design and management perspectives

When discussing PE from a broader management and ergonomic perspective, the concept of "development" or "construction" plays a central role in positioning this type of ergonomic intervention within the processual and systemic quadrants of Whittington's matrix [WHI 01] as well as making the connection with constructive ergonomics (CE). According to Falzon [FAL 15], CE aims to highlight the fact that individuals as well as collectives of operators develop by interacting with the world and by acting upon it. More specifically, similarities between the processual and systemic management approaches, on the one hand, and CE, on the other hand, can be based upon the concept of "capabilities". From a processual strategic management perspective, Mintzberg [MIN 89] introduced "learning and configuration", whereas Teece *et al.* [TEE 97] explained how firm-specific dynamic capabilities are a useful competitive resource but need to be built and redeployed over long periods of time. Whittington [WHI 01], who advocates a systemic strategy perspective, claims that routines applied in local contexts underpin organizational strategy formation processes. The two strategic management perspectives are in line with the "constructive" view on ergonomics, where an optimal compromise between well-being and performance is aimed for [FAL 07]. Following this view, the concept of "enabling environment" has been suggested as a model to integrate various levels of ergonomic action [FAL 05, PAV 07] based upon the idea of "capabilities" [SEN 09]. This enabling environment can be comprehended according to the following three perspectives: preventive, universal and developmental [FAL 15]. With respect to strategic management, the universal and developmental perspective aligns very well with processual and systemic strategies, where individuals in organizations have different interests, deficiencies and opportunities. This means that these individuals are not always united in pursuing economic transactions but act in a network of densely interwoven social relations, so that the organizations they work in are compelled to pursue more pluralistic outcomes [WHI 01].

Robert and Brangier [ROB 09] have extended the meaning of "preventive" to "prospective", emphasizing the "forward-looking in time" aspect (as opposed to retrospection) through the "intelligence analysis" of individual, social, cultural, political, economic, scientific, technological and environmental factors. Relative importance depends on each type of business as well as of multiple data, experts' opinions and scenarios of the future [GOD 96, ROU 06].

However, when considering pluralistic managerial perspectives, PE can also be seen as an extension of CE, where design innovation attempts to emphasize and anticipate human needs and activities so as to create new artifacts that will be useful and provide positive user experience [ROB 09]. The four characteristics of PE are therefore [BRA 12, BRA 14]:

– its user-centeredness, involving the collection of judgments from experts, through, for example, interviews and case studies, as well as from regular users or super users of artifacts: interview, field observation, automatic recording of actions, focus groups, questionnaire, surveys, usability tests, measures of user performance and satisfaction, claim and error analysis, etc.;

– its ability to investigate users' activity through the usage of artifacts in context by aiming to understand (1) what humans are trying to accomplish; (2) what their goals, motivations and underlying needs are; (3) how much time they spend doing these activities; (4) what difficulties or problems they encounter when doing these activities; and (5) how much satisfaction or dissatisfaction they have;

– its ambition to imagine the future by relying on different quantitative and qualitative foresight methods. For example, Gordon and Glenn [GOR 04] classified foresight methods in eight categories according to the goal to be achieved: (1) collect judgment from experts; (2) forecast time series and other quantitative measures; (3) understand the linkages between events, trends and actions; (4) determine a course of action in the presence of uncertainty; (5) portray alternative plausible futures; (6) reach an understanding of whether the future is improving; (7) track changes and assumptions; (8) determine the sustainability of a system; and (9) study the patents in the areas of the innovative projects;

– its position to foster creativity, which lies at the origin of innovation. Hereby, creativity can be defined as the individual or collective capacity to imagine new concepts, objects, products, processes or solutions.

To summarize the differences between PE and CE, one can say that PE carries elements of "creating the external world" in an anticipative mode. This means that PE supports the implementation of processes and methods to innovate new products and services centered around the human and human well-being. CE advocates a constructive and developmental view of ergonomics [FAL 15] The focus is on creating an enabling environment, which takes interest in developing the capabilities of people in organizations as well as preventing detrimental effects on individuals to preserve their future abilities for action [FAL 15, p. x]. When comparing management with ergonomics in general, it can be concluded that there is a strong resemblance between CE and Teece's theory on "dynamic capabilities". However, the way PE distinguishes itself from strategic design on the "human element" demonstrates that PE also shares a similar view that humans are bounded by rationality, to be considered in an innovation and design process. The observation that CE hovers in the systemic and processual quadrants of Whittington's matrix, whereas PE mainly thrives on a systemic strategy, shows that CE is a subset of PE.

After having evaluated selected theoretical frameworks as outlined in this chapter, comparisons according to "orientation", "methods and techniques", "practices" and "value creation" were made between PE and strategic design involving their respective roots, classical ergonomics and strategic management (see Table 3.1). These comparisons are necessary to validate the empirical analysis of cases. The main differences between PE and strategic design are:

– strategic design focuses mainly on business goals in their quest for innovation, whereas PE considers other goals valued by people;

– strategic design emphasizes a positivistic/prescriptive view toward planning, whereas PE is more inclined to accept constructive and participatory innovation and design methods.

	Classical ergonomics (corrective and preventive)	Prospective ergonomics	Strategic design	Strategic management
Orientations	Driven by external legislations and demands	Proactive	Proactive	Proactive
	Focus on current state of affairs (incremental innov. and corr. erg.)	Focus on future products and services	Focus on future products and services	Focus on the future of the organization
	Focus on user and usability issues with respect to product-service system innovation	Product-service system innovation determined by social, economic, political, environmental and technological factors	Product-service system innovation determined by social, economic, political, environmental and technological factors	Focus on organizational innovation
	Contribute to physical and cognitive human well-being	Contribute to business goals by people and for people	Contribute to business goals	Contribute to business goals
	Addresses an existing product or service	Addresses a product or service, which does not exist yet	Applies to an existing and non-existing product or service	Applies to an existing and non-existing product or service

Methods and techniques	User-centered	Human-centered (users, designers, suppliers, distributors, etc.)	Innovation centered, designer centered	Centered around management practices
	Analytical research methods	Prescriptive, analytical, participative and reflective methods	Prescriptive, analytical, participative and reflective methods	Use of deliberate and emergent processes, methods/tools
	Resource-based view	Resource-based view and dynamic capabilities approach	Systematic and prescriptive view toward product planning	Multiple schools of thought
Practices	Considers mainly the user in innovation projects	Considers interest of all stakeholders in innovation projects	Considers mainly the interest of the organization	Considers mainly the interest of the organization
	Human activities are existing and observable	Human activities are prioritized and to be imagined	Human activities not always a priority	Human activities embedded in organizational aims
Value creation	Long-term profitability	Long-term profitability	Long- and short-term profitability	Long and short-term profitability
	Cost reduction through corrective ergonomics	Pluralistic goals in systemic contexts	Profit maximization through increased sales of innovative products and services	Profit maximization through increased sales of innovative products/services and cost reduction

Table 3.1. *Comparison between prospective ergonomics and strategic design involving their respective roots, classical ergonomics and strategic management*

3.2. Ergonomic interventions on management frameworks

In this section, a reflective understanding of PE will be pursued by mapping and discussing different ergonomic domains, interventions and specializations with selected theoretical frameworks, which were addressed earlier in this chapter. More specifically ergonomic domains, interventions and specializations will be reviewed and juxtaposed with the following frameworks:

– classification framework for push-pull innovation perspectives;

– strategy perspectives; process versus outcome [WHI 01];

– Ansoff product – market matrix [ANS 68];

– value creation product/service positioning map [CAG 02];

– design driven innovation framework; meaning versus technology [NOR 12];

– co-creation framework for design research and practice [SAN 08].

3.2.1. *Ergonomic domains, interventions and specializations contextualized within push–pull innovation initiatives*

A fundamental theoretical framework, initiated by market "push–pull" activities and used to contextualize different ergonomic domains, interventions and specializations within strategic management and marketing is shown in Figure 3.1. There are no differences concerning what type of marketing strategy influences typical ergonomic domains and specializations. However, with respect to intervention, corrective ergonomic interventions apply to the market–driven quadrant to facilitate redesign or incremental innovation. Preventive ergonomic intervention targets context-based innovation and is present in all quadrants. Prospective ergonomic intervention is predominantly present in the technology-driven, design-driven and user-driven quadrants, because it aims to solve hidden needs and create new markets, products and services, either deliberate or emergent.

3.2.2. *Ergonomic domains, interventions and specializations contextualized within four strategy perspectives*

Similarities and differences can be observed between generic management strategies and ergonomic domains, interventions and specializations. The axes, indicating process (deliberate–emergent) and outcome (performance–pluralistic), can also be extrapolated for positioning these ergonomic domains, interventions and specializations. With respect to Whittington's generic strategy model, domains and specializations cover a broad spectrum of strategies. However, when juxtapositioning interventions with generic management strategies, the evolutionary and processual approaches limit the scope of corrective or preventive ergonomics, because of their reactive and conservative attitude toward innovation (Figure 3.2). For example, in a processual innovation approach stakeholders may forgo the most promising prospective design solutions because they have not been tested. These stakeholders perceive innovation as a gradual and emergent process of doing things, aimed at plural outcomes. The classical and systemic strategies stimulate more nuanced approaches within PE. PE intervention within the classical quadrant may lead to radical innovation focused upon profit maximization, whereas long-term pluralistic goals are a focal point within a systemic quadrant.

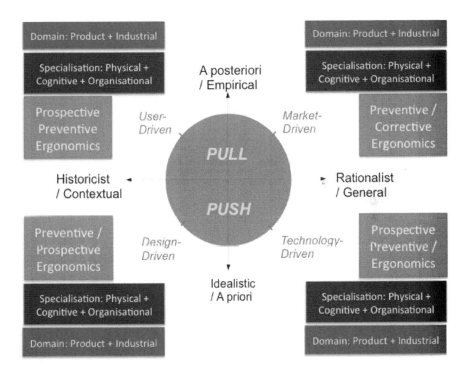

Figure 3.1. *Ergonomic domains, interventions and specializations contextualized within push-pull innovation initiatives*

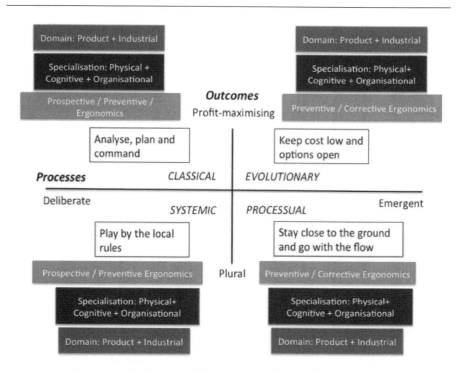

Figure 3.2. *Ergonomic domains, interventions and specializations contextualized within four strategy perspectives*

3.2.3. *Ergonomic domains, interventions and specializations contextualized within Ansoff's product-market matrix*

Technology-based companies are most at ease when objectives and problems are clearly communicated among the project stakeholders through structured product planning and industrial design processes and tools. Ansoff's product-market matrix is an example of a typical prescriptive tool for positioning a company's orientation toward product planning and goal finding. The strategic orientation as depicted in this matrix can also be aligned with ergonomic domains, interventions and specializations (Figure 3.3). In terms of market penetration, product extensions are minimal and most likely limited to aesthetic modifications (face-lifts). Concerning market development, corrective ergonomic measures to improve the hardware and software of products are being emphasized to match users physical and cognitive conditions. When developing new products for existing markets, a more generative approach is being pursued in the development as well as management of products.

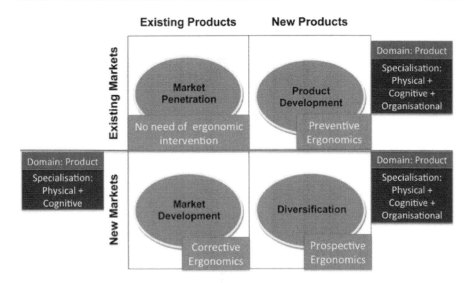

Figure 3.3. *Ergonomic domains, interventions and specializations contextualized within Ansoff's PMT-matrix*

Besides the physical and cognitive, an organizational orientation toward ergonomics is required. The greatest challenge for any company is to diversify, which means developing new products for new markets. In such an approach, the same ergonomic specializations as in "product development" are being emphasized. However, a prospective ergonomic intervention requires designers to adopt a more creative and future-oriented approach toward product development.

3.2.4. *Ergonomic domains, interventions and specializations contextualized within the value creation product positioning map*

As an alternative to Ansoff's PMT-matrix, Cagan and Vogel's positioning map aims to identify products of significant value which integrate "style" (ergonomics and aesthetics) and "technology", so that the company can successfully differentiate itself from the competition. The use of this prescriptive method facilitates (1) the identification of product opportunities, (2) the translation of consumer needs into actionable insights and defined attributes and (3) the integration of engineering, industrial design and marketing.

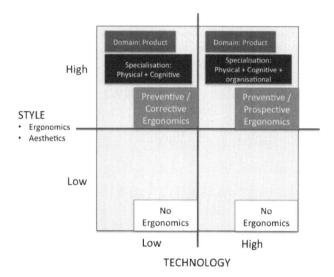

Figure 3.4. *Ergonomic domains, interventions and specializations contextualized within the value creation product positioning map (adapted from [CAG 02])*

Ergonomic specializations are mainly physical and cognitive in the high "style" quadrants but are extended to organizational where high "technology" and "style" meet. Ergonomic intervention is limited to corrective or preventive if a product is designed based on existing technology. However, with respect to value creation in the high "style" and high "technology" quadrant, a prospective ergonomic perspective facilitates the development of creative breakthrough ideas, which are initiated and emerge from daily activities, where people are operating in embedded contexts of culture, workplace, family, etc.

3.2.5. *Ergonomic domains, interventions and specializations contextualized within design-driven innovation*

A design-driven framework, where incremental and radical innovations are reflected against technology and meaning change, is shown in Figure 3.5. More specifically, the framework connects the two dimensions of innovation (technology and meaning) with the drivers: technology, design and users (the market). These two dimensions were used to define four types of innovations [VER 08]: technology-push, meaning-driven, technology epiphanies and market-pull.

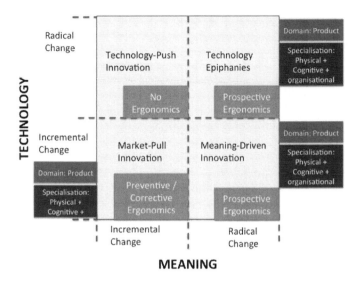

Figure 3.5. *Ergonomic domains, interventions and specializations contextualized within design-driven innovation*

1) *Technology-push innovation* comes from radical changes in technology without any change in the meaning of products. The invention of the digital camera (on top of the existing conventional ones) is an example. Technology-push innovations are definitely not derived from users' insights [CHR 13, DOS 82].

2) *Meaning-driven innovation* starts from the discernment of subtle and unspoken dynamics in sociocultural contexts, resulting in radically new meanings and languages, which often imply a change in sociocultural regimes. The invention of the miniskirt in the 1960s is an example: not simply a different skirt but a radically new symbol of women's freedom that recognized a radical change in society. Moreover, the "Tupperware Party Direct Sale" concept instigated a cultural revolution in post-World War II America. It was not just about selling plastic kitchen containers to store food but rather a manifestation of radically feminized articulations of women's freedom. In both examples, no new technology was involved.

3) Enabled by the emergence of new technologies or the use of existing technologies in totally new contexts, *technology epiphanies* bring a radical change in meaning. The Wii video game console and the Swatch watch are examples of this type of innovation. The term "epiphany" is to be

comprehended as "a meaning that exists at a superior level" and a "vehicle that embraced the essential nature or meaning of something". This superior application of a technology is often not visible at first, because it does not satisfy existing needs. It does not come from users. Rather, the dominant interpretation of what a product should be is derived from a latent meaning that is revealed only when new and unsolicited products that people are not currently seeking are being designed [VER 11, VER 13].

4) *Market-pull innovation* starts from an analysis of user needs and then develops products to satisfy them.

Although human behavior may be influenced, technology push does not purposely introduce significant ergonomic interventions. In the example of the digital camera, users' behavior in taking pictures has changed significantly but ease of use and ergonomic efficiency were initially not targeted. In "market-pull innovation", corrective or preventive ergonomics influence the design of products and services, which have been driven by users' needs. In market-driven innovation and technology epiphanies, a prospective ergonomic approach to the design of products and services may lead to the most innovative solutions. These innovative solutions may target the physical and cognitive design of the new product, its complementary service processes and scenarios, as well as the organization and production set up to realize these new products.

3.2.6. *Ergonomic interventions contextualized within a co-creation framework for design research and practice*

Within design practice, significant efforts have been concentrated on user-centered design methods to develop and analyze future scenarios [VER 05]. At the same time, design researchers distinguish between traditional experimental methods and design-study methods (e.g. narrative accounts and interpretive frameworks), broadening the debate on positivist and "postpositivist" science and advocating the need for a new epistemology that meets the needs of "human sciences" [PHI 00].

According to Figure 3.6, a strong inclination can be observed in the design and use of methods and tools which promote the anticipation and creative development of prospective products and services with or without the participative involvement of different stakeholders. Hereby, the role of the designer can be twofold: facilitative, by being able to manage participatory design sessions, as well as visionary, by being able to imagine future products and services and convince lead-users to accept them through a hermeneutic way of design reasoning [LIE 14, p. 100].

With respect to a critical and emotional design, an expert visionary mindset and design-led approach may address ergonomic intervention of products at different levels: corrective, preventive and prospective. The level of intervention is dependent on the problem space and context. Moving to an expert mindset and research-led approach, user-centered design practices promote incremental innovation through corrective and preventive ergonomic interventions. The use of generative methods and tools, which facilitate a partially design and research-led approach combined with a participatory mindset, is most suitable for stimulating PE in the design of new products and services, where insights from a wider range of stakeholders are considered to be indispensable.

In Figure 3.6, PE thrives on certain combinations of mindsets and design approaches. These combinations are as follows:

– on a hermeneutic note, where the designer is considered an expert, who has a vision of the future;

– on a participatory note, where the designer is a facilitator, who mobilizes a broad range of stakeholders to create the future and discover hidden needs.

In this chapter, ergonomic domains, specializations and interventions have been contextualized against different strategy and innovation frameworks to position the field of PE.

From a strategic management and design reasoning perspective, PE can be characterized as follows:

– PE targets various aspects of "innovation": aesthetic (hedonistic/emotional), user-functional, service, etc. However, it complements the more "radical" views on innovation as depicted in Figures 3.3–3.5;

– generic strategies are important to anticipate and imagine implicit needs and wants, as well as to create future solutions which have not been identified yet;

– based upon the type of problem, context, company objectives and stakeholders expertise ergonomists, designers and business managers should jointly decide what type of generic strategy, as well as design processes and methods to adopt. Additionally, social, technological, economical, environmental and political factors are important contextual determinants, which should be included if plural objectives are to be met through a systemic way of strategizing and designing;

– from a design perspective, the use of human-centered approaches should be balanced as well as critically advanced by design-driven methods and tools. In this context, the input from experts outside the realm of direct users can lead to even more surprising and creative solutions.

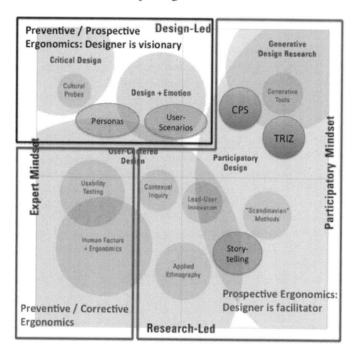

Figure 3.6. *Ergonomic interventions contextualized within a co-creation framework of design research and practice (adapted from [SAN 08])*

3.3. Summary

The main aim behind the theoretical part of this work is to communicate that strategic management perspectives on innovation as well as strategic design principles extend the field of PE. Pure positivism does not represent a PE approach in developing new products and services. Instead, a combination of positivist and constructivist worldviews is fundamental for adopting PE in a systemic strategy context. Both systemic strategizing and PE acknowledge that innovating is a complex activity bounded by social, technological, economic, environmental and political constraints, which may lead to plural outcomes.

Prior to making an argument for extending PE, this new field of ergonomics was contextualized within and aligned with theories and frameworks of innovation and strategic design. As prospective ergonomics targets various aspects of "innovation" (aesthetic (hedonistic/emotional), user-functional, service, etc.), different prescriptive positioning exercises are valuable for the anticipation and imagination of implicit needs and wants as well as to create prospective design solutions.

Prioritizing the well-being of people, important contextual determinants to be considered for promoting the innovation and creative aspects of prospective ergonomics are based on social, technological, economical, environmental and political factors. If plural objectives are to be met through a systemic way of strategizing and designing, ergonomists, designers and business managers should adopt a comprehensive prospective ergonomic approach based upon the type of problem, context, company objectives and stakeholders involvement.

The theoretical foundation of this work is supported by 12 case studies, which are reported, discussed and cross-compared in Chapters 5 and 6. Figure 3.7 shows the alignments between different levels of ergonomic and design interventions within strategic management.

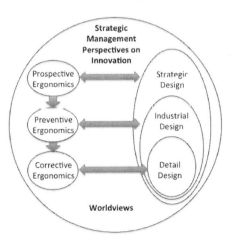

Figure 3.7. *Alignments and differences between compatible macroergonomic and strategic management perspectives at different levels of comprehensiveness*

Research Organization

4.1. Overview

In this chapter, an argument is made to use retrospective case study research for answering empirical data that has been constructed from selected cases, exemplified in the author's previous articles. Moreover, a choice is made to use the term research organization rather than "research method" in characterizing this chapter. A "within-case analysis" is proposed to critically reflect on the processes, methods and results for each case according to the following dimensions: orientation, method, practice and value creation. Hereby, ergonomic and design interventions, as well as units of analysis and dimensions, are deduced from the theoretical framework and concepts. Following the within-case analysis, a cross-case analysis is used to compare cases within and across the quadrants. Using a cross-case comparison, subtle similarities and differences between cases are sought after. The juxtaposition of similar cases dissects simplistic frames, while the search for similarities in seemingly different pairs leads to a more sophisticated understanding of prospective ergonomics (PE). As a result, forced comparisons reveals new methods, products and services, which the investigator did not anticipate.

Since the aim of this work is to outline and frame the field of PE influenced by established ergonomic perspectives (corrective/preventive), strategic management, as well as strategic and industrial design concepts, relationships are drawn with knowledge fields in ergonomics, business management, innovation and design sciences to complement theory building in PE. This means that the attention of the ergonomic and design community may need to be drawn upon to develop new approaches, models and methods to redefine the field of ergonomics to be more proactive and prospective.

Furthermore, this work also attempts to build upon different generic business strategies and design reasoning modes, which in turn function as a classification framework for positioning various business, ergonomic, and design methods and tools.

The redefinition of innovation-driven PE from a strategic management and different ergonomic and design interventions have led to the following research questions:

– What are the similarities and differences in terms of attitudes and approaches between PE and strategic design, preventive ergonomics and industrial design, corrective ergonomics and detail design?

– From a pluralistic business strategy perspective, does the balancing of performance/productivity, on the one hand, and well-being, on the other hand, supports the spirit of PE?

– Does a systemic business strategy, supported by a structured user-centered and context-driven design approach, represents the field of PE in the development of innovative products, systems and services?

– To what extent are prescriptive approaches, methods and tools applicable for solving strategic design problems within the context of PE?

– What are the possible design education strategies, processes, methods and tools to be considered for PE and strategic design issues?

Because this emergent piece of work is constructed from a selection of articles, written throughout the author's academic career of 20 years, it is more suitable to use the term research organization rather than "research method" to characterize this chapter. The empirical data have been constructed from selected cases, which were embedded in the selected articles. A two-stage process was used to classify the cases. In the first stage, cases were categorized according to ergonomic and design interventions as shown in Table 3.1. In the second stage, the cases were mapped according to generic strategies, worldviews and models of design reasoning to be analyzed according to the following dimensions: "orientation", "method", "practice" and "value creation". The mapping is shown in section 6.5 as part of the case cluster comparison across the four quadrants.

4.2. What is case study research and how can it be applied here?

Case study research is a strategy, which focuses on understanding the dynamics present within single settings. It can be used to accomplish various aims: to provide description [KID 82], test theory [PIN 86] or generate theory [GER 88, HAR 86]. Evidence from case studies, which may be qualitative, quantitative, or both, are typically derived from combining data collection methods such as archives, interviews, documented project work and observations [YIN 84]. Because the aim of this work is to relate selected theories from philosophy, innovation management and design to create epistemologies on PE, selected cases have been chosen based on the concept of "appropriate population", which means that a set of entities from which the research sample is drawn is defined by the population.

Sampling of cases from the chosen population is a common practice when building theory from case studies and depends on theoretical sampling (i.e. cases are chosen for theoretical, not statistical reasons [GLA 67]). The cases may be selected to replicate previous cases or develop emergent theory, or they may be chosen to substantiate theoretical categories and provide examples of polar types [EIS 89]. While the cases may be chosen randomly, in some cases it may be preferable to choose the cases selectively.

According to Pettigrew [PET 88], given the limited number of cases, which can usually be studied in extending emergent theories, it makes sense to choose cases based upon extreme situations where diverse interests are "clearly observable". However, for this work, the author adopts a broader view in selecting typical practice-derived cases, which are relevant for building theory.

Frequent iterations between data analysis and data collection is a striking feature of theory building through case studies research. For example, with respect to a grounded theory approach, Glaser and Strauss [GLA 67] argue for joint collection, coding and analysis of data, which not only gives the researcher an analytical head start, but essentially allows researchers to take advantage of flexible data collection. Moreover, the freedom to make adjustments during the data collection process is a typical key feature of theory building in case study research. Hereby, adjustments can be made through the addition of cases to probe particular themes or strengthen the argument of the author, whether, for example, to support or decline an emergent phenomenon.

As the cases presented in this dissertation were selected from the author's past and diverse research and project work, a retrospective case study method has been adopted in conjunction with a within-case analysis approach [PET 88, THO 11].

Within-case analysis typically involves writing-up each case in a detailed and descriptive manner to generate key insights [GER 88, PET 88]. However, there is no standard format for analysis, because the volume of data is a compilation of the author's previous articles.

The objective of adopting a within-case analysis for this work is to become intimately familiar with each case as stand-alone entity. The benefits of using "within-case analysis" are that unique patterns of each case are made to emerge before investigators generalize patterns across cases (cross-case analysis). In this work, a within-case analysis was conducted by critically reflecting on the processes, methods and results for each case according to the following dimensions: orientation, method, practice and value creation. Dimensions were deduced from theoretical frameworks and concepts, and can be seen as a customized format for analyzing the cases.

Following the within-case analysis, a cross-case analysis will be conducted based on a two-stage process. In the first stage, cases will be compared within their respective quadrants, whereas in the second stage case clusters are to be compared across quadrants of the generic strategy framework [WHI 01].

Using a within-case comparison, subtle similarities and differences between cases are sought after. The juxtaposition of seemingly similar cases by a researcher looking for differences can break simplistic frames [EIS 89, p. 541]. Equivalently, searching for similarity in a seemingly different pair also can lead to a more sophisticated understanding of PE. The result of making forced comparisons can lead to new categories and concepts, which the investigator was not able to foresee. Cross-case searching tactics may enhance the probability of capturing the novel findings, which may exist in the data as represented by the cases. The application of cross-case searching tactics seems to be effective in encouraging the investigator to go beyond initial impressions, especially by using structured and diverse lenses on the data. These tactics improve the likelihood of accurate and reliable theory. Furthermore, the central idea is that researchers constantly compare and conjecture between theory and data to sharpen the construct. In research, a construct is the abstract idea, underlying theme, hypothesis, research question or subject matter that one wishes to measure. Theory building is usually a two-part process involving (1) refining the definition of the construct and (2) building evidence that measures the construct in each case. This occurs through constant comparison between data and constructs so that accumulating evidence from diverse sources converges on a single, well-defined construct [EIS 89, p. 541].

4.3. Description and interpretation of dimensions of analysis

In the study of each individual case, "orientation", "model of design reasoning", "practice" and value creation" will be used as the dimensions of analysis. "Orientation" can be defined as the positioning of the cases according to ergonomic and design intervention, worldview and relationship to the broader context of strategizing. "Method" concerns the approach on how the concept is being addressed or realized. However, the objectives as put forward in some of the cases can also be a process or method in itself. The dimension practice frames the activities of the actors and stakeholders involved in the design and development processes of the respective cases.

From a technology perspective, value creation can be seen as a motivator to create new possibilities and solutions as well as to make cost reductions on a solution to an existing problem [CHE 02]. Moreover, this fourth dimension, "value" should not exclusively be appreciated from a monetary perspective. Neither involvement or four perspectives on value is a suitable framework for analyzing the contribution of each of the selected cases as it does not only reside in the product purchased, in the brand chosen, or the object possessed, but rather in the experience(s) of interacting with it [HOL 99, p. 8]. As argued by Den Ouden [DEN 11], the value of a product or service is not a property that can be directly measured scientifically, like other properties such as weight or volume. It should be a relational property that only exists in relation to a human. In this context, it is therefore more important to deeply understand the motivational values of the various stakeholders, especially for innovations that aim to change user behavior [FOG 09]. The value creation model as elaborated by den Ouden (2011) according to four levels of stakeholder involvement and four perspectives on value, is a suitable framework for analysing the contribution of each of the selected cases.

4.4. Preparing cases and summarizing terminologies; worldviews, modes of design reasoning, generic strategies and interventions

In the last sections of Chapter 5, all cases will be evaluated according to applied worldviews, design reasoning modes and generic strategies, as well as cross-analyzed based on different types of ergonomic and design interventions. In addition, each of the cases will specifically be analyzed according to worldview and design reasoning mode. Finally, all the cases will be compared on how we intervene in them from a design as well as from an ergonomic perspective.

Before embarking on the different forms of case study analysis, which are outlined in Chapters 4 and 5, a summary of the different terms will be given below:

– philosophical worldviews with respect to design research and designing can be interpreted as a way of scientifically explaining the different mindsets, attitudes and perspectives in developing new products and services;

– design reasoning modes are designers' intellectual and practice-oriented stances toward how the design of products and services should be executed;

– according to Whittington [WHI 01], generic strategies describe the options, which are available for a company to pursue competitive advantage in the "real World", either by aiming for profit maximizing or plural outcomes. To achieve these outcomes, the company may use deliberate/structured processes or emergent ones;

– PE can be defined as the part of ergonomics that attempts to anticipate and create new and useful artifacts, based on human needs and activities, so as to provide positive user experience [ROB 09]. The anticipation of human needs and activities is derived from analyzing numerous factors and data as well as scenario planning, done in prospection. This implies that individual, social, cultural, political, economic, scientific, technological and environmental factors should be considered when proposing future human-centered innovations. Its multidisciplinary nature justifies the use of a wide range of theories, models, methods and tools from the human and social sciences;

– strategic design is a field of study and practice, where different actors are involved in planning and generating integrated systems of products, services and communications that are coherent with the medium-and long-term perspective of sustainable innovations, being, at the same time, economically feasible and socially applicable today [MAN 03]. Its intention is to develop ways to address these medium- and long-term goals based on new forms of organizations, new systems of values, new stakeholder configurations and new market opportunities;

– in conceptual or industrial design, both applied art and applied science are used to improve aesthetic, ergonomic and technical functionality, and/or usability of a product. Furthermore, it may also be used to improve the product's marketability and even production. In this context, the role of an industrial designer is to solve problems, create and execute design solutions with respect to form, usability, physical ergonomics, marketing, brand development and sales [NOB 93];

– preventive ergonomics is the science of fitting the task to the user to avoid a mismatch between the physical requirements of the activity and the physical capacity of the user. It encompasses the practice of designing equipment, tools and work tasks to conform to the capability of this user (*Ergonomics and the Prevention of Work-Related Musculoskeletal Disorders. Department of Health, New Jersey, http://nj.gov/health/peosh/ergonomics.shtml. retrieved 11.03.2014*);

– detail design is the phase where the design is refined by optimizing ergonomic, aesthetic, technological, marketing and environmental solutions, which were earlier proposed in the design conceptualization stages of the process. In practice, plans, specifications and estimates are created for prospective manufacturing. The output of detailed design activities includes 2D and 3D models, prototypes, cost build up estimates, procurement plans, etc. In this phase, a majority of the project expenses will be consumed;

– corrective ergonomics is reactive and deals with correcting existing artifacts through scientific studies [MON 67, LAU 86].

Analysis of 12 Design Case Studies

5.1. Introduction

In this chapter, a "within case study" analysis has been performed, where each case has been reflected upon based on the following dimensions: orientation, method, practice and value creation. A retrospective case study research method has been used for building a more succinct understanding of the differences and similarities between prospective ergonomics and strategic design, as well as their superior and subordinate levels of embodiments. The cases were grouped and analyzed according to ergonomic intervention and structurally presented to facilitate cross-comparisons in Chapter 6.

5.2. Analysis of cases within corrective ergonomic intervention

In this section, the following cases will be discussed within the context of corrective ergonomic intervention:

– USB-memory stick for customer recruitment;

– anthropometric considerations for embarkation and disembarkation at bus shelters;

– digital human models in work system design and simulation.

5.2.1. *USB memory stick for customer recruitment (USB)*

In this "Lady's Card" credit card campaign, the United Overseas Bank of Singapore (UOB) commissioned the design and development of a USB memory stick to recruit female applicants. The manufacturing of the memory stick was realized by Valen Technologies, through the purchase the electronics and molding of plastic parts at significantly affordable prices. This made it attractive for UOB to purchase large quantities to be distributed as gift for successful female credit card applicants.

A constructive/pragmatic worldview has been adopted in the redesign of a low-cost version of a USB memory stick. The redesign was reactive and initiated from the emerging opportunity to develop a device, which is affordable to be distributed as a gift. Corrective interventions were aimed at facilitating strategic design motivations.

General characteristics	Aim/context		Lady's card credit card campaign for the recruitment of female applicants	
	Publication		*Results of the project have been extensively used for teaching purposes*	
Project organization	Duration of project		March 2002–July 2002 (5 months)	
	Actors/stakeholders		United Overseas Bank of Singapore (UOB), Valen Technologies and their suppliers	
Dimensions of analysis	Orientation	Positioning	Domain	Product/service
			Specialization	Physical
			Intervention	Corrective Erg. – strategic design
		Worldview	Constructivist/pragmatic	
		Generic strategy	Evolutionary/processual	
	Design reasoning model and method		Reflective practice	
	Practice		Industrial design and design detailing	
	Value creation		Build and enlargement of customer base	

In the design process, a reflective approach was adopted in the conceptualization of the USB stick. It was incidental that Valen Technologies was able to source the electronics at a relatively low cost from a Taiwanese supplier. (*At that time, in 2003, USB technology was expensive and newly patented, but as Taiwanese manufacturers were not subjected to intellectual property rules and regulations, they were able to copy unrestrictedly*). The oval shape of the electronics also suggested the presence of symmetry lines, which were used as a reference for developing symmetrical plastic parts, saving tooling costs.

From a business and value creation perspective, this project can be characterized as processual. In the collaboration between Valen Technologies and UOB, direct sales and profit maximization were not targeted with the USB sticks. Instead, the business model was to use the USB stick as a means for enticing prospective female credit card customers. Moreover, the incidentally low manufacturing cost was also a characteristic of an emergent process.

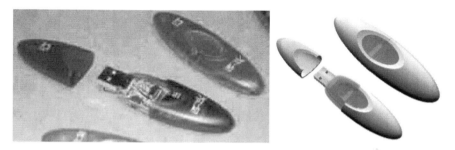

Figure 5.1. *Low-cost USB memory stick for enticing prospective credit card customers*

5.2.2 *Anthropometric considerations for embarkation and disembarkation at bus shelters (BUS SHELTER)*

In Singapore, improvements on bus shelters are based on a checklist provided by the Land Transport Authority of Singapore (LTA), which was adapted from British Standards, disregarding the differences in anthropometric profiles of the population and local climate. The interface between bus shelter and bus: embarkation and disembarkation, was an important issues to be dealt with, because of the high flux of users at bus shelters in Singapore. In the period of 2000–2004, the LTA was in the process of replacing their bus shelters island wide. Hence, this anthropometric study is a project undertaken to investigate the ease of embarkation and disembarkation from bus to bus shelters and vice versa.

Most often it was necessary to take account of the tallest persons to decide on legroom or shortest persons to make sure they can navigate gaps between road curb and bus platform safely and comfortably. In terms of orientation, the predefined and research-driven nature of this project demanded a positivistic worldview toward problem solving. A corrective ergonomic approach was pursued in this project as embarkation and disembarkation from bus to bus shelters were existing and common phenomena.

General characteristics	Aim/context		To improve the interface between bus shelter and bus for embarkation and disembarkation	
	Publication		Liem, André; Hu Xia, "Anthropometric considerations for embarkation and disembarkation at bus shelters", SEAMEC Conference, Conference Proceedings; Kuching, Malaysia, 2003.	
Organization of the project	Duration of project		August 2001–August 2003	
	Actors/stakeholders		Land Transport Authority of Singapore (LTA) National University of Singapore, Department of Architecture (NUS-ARCH)	
Dimensions of analysis	Orientation	Positioning	Domain	Product
			Specialization	Physical
			Intervention	Corrective Erg. – Industrial Design
		Worldview	Positivistic	
	Generic strategy		Classical	
	Design reasoning models and methods		Problem solving, Research methods: Interviews, observations	
	Practice		Anthropometric research for design	
	Value creation		Development of design insights and guidelines	

Since the purpose of this study was to investigate the proposition that anthropometric characteristics of Singaporeans affect the ease of embarkation and disembarkation from bus to bus shelters, methods such as observations and interviews were used to determine the ideal distance between road curb and bus platform.

As research dominated the practice component in this project, recommendations to enhance the design of bus shelters were derived from overall static anthropometric data of the distances between curbs to bus platforms. One hundred and twenty healthy subjects participated in anthropometric measurements. Results indicated that although embarkation showed a laterally inverted relationship with disembarkation, assumptions that body movement mechanics are the same for both embarkation and disembarkation should not be made. Derivation of the "recommended" distances from the static and sampling stick figure was accomplished by considering maxima, minima and general recommendations from literature. However, because of the complex interaction between the various dimensions it was very unlikely that the "recommended" distances would prove to be entirely satisfactory in practice. From a value and stakeholder's perspective, the outcome of the research contributes to architects' and LTAs' insights in designing universally accessible workshops.

Figure 5.2. *Covered video observation still capture with stick figure superimposed on user*

5.2.3. *Digital human models in work system design and simulation (DHM)*

This work presents the application of digital human models in the simulation of downtown baggage check-in system at City Hall Mass Rapid Transit (MRT) station in Singapore. The challenge was to integrate the simulation of the personnel, technical and environmental subsystems into one computer model, which allows researchers from different disciplines to easily understand and discuss the system design. The application of digital human modeling also introduced another perspective to describe the body ellipse theory and queuing level-of-service standards. Body ellipse templates and queuing level-of-service standards were applied to locate and determine workspaces of the digital human models in the air passengers' check-in queuing simulation. The locations of human models, instead of being manipulated by the hinge points on the bodies, were manipulated by virtual points such as the quadrant points of the ellipse outside the body. Their interpersonal space was therefore decided by the clearance between the quadrant points of the body ellipses. In parallel, a human model with the baggage/trolley can be considered as one integral block. They were positioned and managed by manipulating the endpoints on the boundary lines of the block.

General characteristics	Aim/context	To improve design efficiency through the use of Digital Human Models in Work System Design and Simulation		
	Publication	Liem, André; Huang Yan, "Digital human models in work system design and simulation", SAE 2004, In Proceedings of Digital Human Modelling for Design and Engineering Symposium, Oakland University, Rochester, MI		
Organization of the project	Duration of project	August 2001–August 2003		
	Actors/stakeholders	Mass Rapid Transport Authorities of Singapore (MRT-Singapore) National University of Singapore, Department of Architecture (NUS-ARCH)		
Dimensions of analysis	Orientation	Positioning	Domain	Product
			Specialization	Cognitive
			Intervention	Corrective Erg. – Industrial/detail design
		Worldview	Positivistic	
		Generic strategy	Classical	
		Design reasoning model and method	Problem solving	
		Practice	Ergonomic research and design	
		Value creation	Development of design insights and guidelines Enhancement of the business ecosystem	

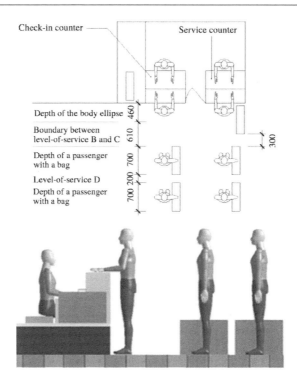

Figure 5.3. *The simulation of check-in queues at the Singapore MRT station*

The orientation of this project was based upon a positivist worldview, where classical and problem solving principles were adopted to correctively intervene in the ergonomic (re)design using work system simulations involving human models and objects. In terms of methods and tools, the use of CAD made it relatively convenient to manipulate the spatial relationships among the digital human models, the check-in facilities and the workplace as well as the external environments.

Considering practice, researchers, designers and other stakeholders with different backgrounds collaborated in the design of a downtown check-in work system. Collaboration wise, the use of digital human models would be a suitable platform to design, assess and communicate the project. The CAD simulation, which integrated subjects, check-in facilities, and the MRT station workplace, created a valuable platform for decision makers and stakeholders with respect to understanding and communicating the flow and mechanisms of the work system.

5.3. Analysis of cases within preventive ergonomic intervention

In this section, the following cases will be discussed within the context of corrective ergonomic intervention:

– mail production: the Norwegian Postal Service (NPS);

– classroom system for elementary school pupils;

– interior concepts for small space living;

– interior customization of Singapore fast-response police car;

– rucksack bag design to facilitate optimum loading.

5.3.1. *Mail production: the NPS*

General characteristics	Aim/context		To improve mail production and delivery through systems design.	
	Publication		Liem, André, "Teaching strategic and systems design to facilitate collaboration and learning", FORMakademisk, vol. 5, no. 1, pp. 29–48, 2012.	
Organization of the project	Duration of project		January 2005–May 2005 (5 Months)	
	Actors/stakeholders		Norwegian Postal Service (NPS); Norwegian University of Science and Technology (NTNU); Inventas AS	
Dimensions of analysis	Orientation	Positioning	Domain	Industrial ergonomics
			Specialization	Physical, cognitive, organizational
			Intervention	Preventive Erg.– Systems Design
		Worldview		Positivistic
		Generic strategy		Classical
	Design reasoning model and method		Problem solving, structured designing processes	
	Practice		Ergonomic systems design and industrial design	
	Value creation		– Cost savings and profit enhancement for Norwegian Postal service	
			– Improved industrial ergonomic processes	

In the NPS project, a systems approach was implemented in the design of a mail distribution service. In this project, the system is the collection of subsystems and products, whereas the structure is the predetermined and fundamental logistic framework on which this mail distribution system is based upon. The term structure is diachronous in nature, which means that the relationships are time and sequence dependent.

The aim was to expose students to complex design thinking situations at an early stage of their education. In the first stage, several system alternatives were iteratively generated and evaluated through a series of scenario and task analyses, which were elaborated into a feasible and detailed system concept.

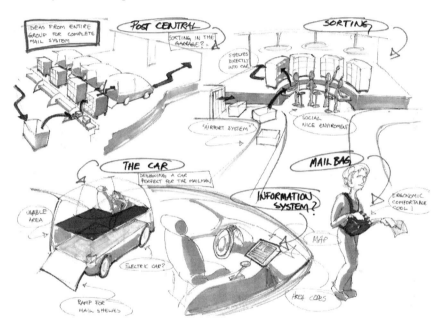

Figure 5.1. A systems approach in the development of mail production and distribution concept, considering market and technological developments

In the second stage, students further developed subsystems and products into two or three detailed design concepts. The selected design concept was then subjected to several rounds of refinement, user testing and materialization.

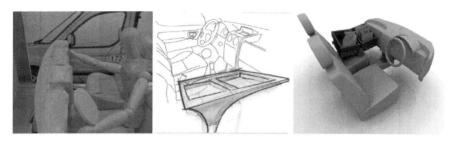

Figure 5.5. *(a–c) Analysis and concept development
of a front-seat mail sorter*

The final stage was an extension of the studio, whereby selected designs were commissioned by NPS for further development and professional prototyping.

Figure 5.6. *(a–c) Examples of user testing and detailing
and prototype development*

In terms of orientation, this NPD project was managed using structured designing processes supported by a positivistic worldview. As the problem space has already been defined, ergonomic interventions were preventive in nature. The overall system addressed many organizational ergonomic issues through people-to-people and people-to-machine interactions, whereas subordinate systems and products were either physically or cognitively rich in content.

Building upon Savransky's [SAV 00] systems thinking approach, complex design projects involving many elements and stakeholders can be structured and managed according to a hierarchical and systematic way of project organization.

Within the overarching NPS mail production system, such a systems thinking approach can be an effective generator for extending the creativity space leading to the creation of ancillary and complementary design projects as well as broadening the network of stakeholders.

In terms of value creation, cost savings and profit enhancement for the Norwegian Postal service have been targeted.

5.3.2. *Classroom system for elementary school students (Classr. Sys.)*

General characteristics	Aim/context		To design an elementary classroom system	
	Publication		Liem, André, "Teaching strategic and systems design to facilitate collaboration and learning", FORMakademisk, vol. 5, no. 1, pp. 29–48, 2012.	
Organization of the project	Duration of project		January 2010–May 2010 (5 months)	
	Actors/stakeholders		– Moelven AS	
			– Norwegian University of Science & Technology	
Dimensions of analysis	Orientation	Positioning	Domain	Product ergonomics
			Specialization	Physical
			Intervention	Preventive Erg. – Systems Design
		Worldview	Positivistic	
		Generic Strategy	Systemic	
	Design reasoning model and method		Problem solving, hermeneutic, reflective practice	
	Practice		Ergonomic systems design and industrial design	
	Value creation		Enhancement of product portfolio and profit	
			New insights into organizing design studio teaching	

This project shows the design of an interior classroom setup for elementary school pupils using a system design perspective. In the product conceptualization and detailing stages, each group member took responsibility of a system element. In general, this group, comprising second- and third-grade design students, was successful in determining the system as well as the shared boundaries among the elements.

Strong leadership qualities among the third-grade members contributed to the clarity of design tasks. However, in the detailing and materialization stage, more time and effort than expected was spent in fine-tuning and making sure that the elements interact in a coherent manner. This demonstrated the presence of an overcompassing iterative process between system and product/element design.

A strict design process supported by a problem solving and design reasoning attitude was essential to achieve the design objectives within a systemic strategic context [SIM 96, WHI 01]. Also, a positivistic philosophical worldview was adopted in the planning and structuring of the vertical studio project to facilitate a methodology based upon a hierarchical mentorship-driven way of learning. Hereby, the interactions among group members, teachers and collaborating companies facilitated "reflective" [SCH 95] and "hermeneutic" [BAM 02, SNO 92, DAR 79] thinking to complement a problem solving oriented way of designing. In terms of practice, ergonomic systems design and industrial design contributed to the structured planning of the vertical studio. Value is created through the enhancement of Moelven's product portfolio and profit as well as new insights into organizing studio design teaching.

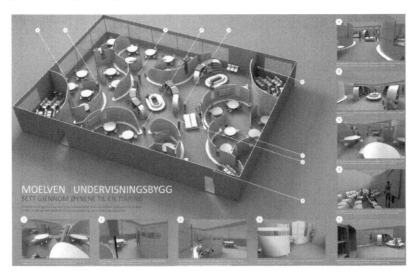

Figure 5.7. *An example of an interior classroom setup for elementary school pupils, designed from a systems and product perspective*

5.3.3. *Interior concepts for small-space living (ICSSL)*

General characteristics	Aim/context		How to create an optimal balance between living space, storage facilities and comfort through accessibility of items/equipment	
	Publication		Liem, André, "Development of interior concepts to facilitate small-space living in Singapore", Journal of Southeast Asian Architecture, vol. 7, pp. 47–57, 2004.	
Organization of the project	Duration of project		January 1999–December 1999 (12 Months)	
	Actors/stakeholders		Singapore Housing Development Board (HDB) National University of Singapore (NUS-ARCH)	
Dimensions of analysis	Orientation	Positioning	Domain	Product ergonomics
			Specialization	Physical
			Intervention	Preventive – Systems Design
		Worldview	Positivistic	
		Generic strategy		Systemic
	Design reasoning model and method		Problem solving, hermeneutic, reflective practice	
	Practice		Ergonomic systems design and industrial design	
	Value creation		Happiness/eco-footprint	

Increasingly, *indented walls* and *higher ceilings* are becoming more common in the construction of apartment housing in Singapore. These higher ceilings and indented walls created opportunities in the development of interior concepts for small-space living and Do-It-Yourself (DIY) furniture concepts. Instead of removing non-supporting walls, which is a costly exercise, one alternative for space creation is to make full use of the intricate corners, indented spaces (Figure 5.8) and if possible, internal height of its units. For example, regarding the 130 cm long IKEA Lack shelves, the buyer had to shorten the shelves (by sawing) to fit them into a 120 cm wide indentation. This was a tedious and time-consuming task, and the construction of the shelf itself was significantly weakened.

Figure 5.8. *An example of indented walls in Singapore apartment housing*

A flexible shelf system (Figure 5.9), which can be extended in length and depth, was proposed to optimize the space in-between indented walls. The design was based on a mechanism whereby standard parts slide among each other. This sliding mechanism, with the possibility of adding standard parts, allows the shelf to form any desired length–width ratio, meeting the need of exactly fitting the shelf into any width of indented wall. In this way, the sides of the indentation can also be used to provide a supportive function, for example to keep books from falling sideways. Each shelf is supported by internal extendable metal bars, which can be adjusted according to the desired depth (see illustration).

A preventive ergonomic and systems design approach has been adopted in the design of this piece of furniture. As the physical context (interior environment) and presumed lifestyles have been determined, this project can be characterized as systemic. Structured problem solving processes and methods were used, complemented by hermeneutic and reflective dispositions in design reasoning, because of the project's systemic nature. Complementary to its constructive and ergonomic focus in the project, the designer aimed to develop interior solutions that are aesthetically pleasing, affordable, high quality, space efficient and easy for the consumer to install (DIY home solutions).

In this interior design project, a systematic design process has been used, which is very much context driven. The value in such a systemic project is twofold. In terms of the design solution, it advocates collaboration between industrial designers, interior designers and architects. With respect to design thinking, this project contributed to students' awareness and sensitivity toward appreciating certain cultural contexts.

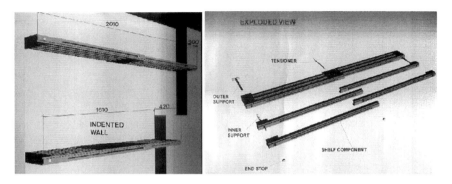

Figure 5.9. *The "flexible shelf" consists of standard components to be assembled to achieve any desired width–length ratio*

5.3.4. *Interior customization of Singapore fast-response police car (ICSFRC)*

In 2001, the Singapore Police Force (SPF) launched initiatives to improve and enhance the installation and use of equipment to optimize its fast response operations using police patrol vehicles with in-vehicle information and communication systems. Fast response cars, such as ambulances, fire engines and police vehicles, respond to emergency hotline (999 in Singapore) calls and all incidents reported by members of the public and Police Head Quarters.

Mandatory elements include the positioning of an on-board computer terminal and keyboard, radio and data transfer communication equipment in the front area of the vehicle, as well as efficient storage of other equipment and tools required for fast-response operations, such as bolt cutter, roadblock signs, riot shields, etc., in the rear area of the vehicle.

In the design and development of special vehicles, such as police cars, fire engines and ambulances, two different approaches can be identified in the interior design and customization of these vehicles. The first is defined as vehicle integrative customization and the second as vehicle adaptive customization. Integrative customization in vehicle design is the implementation of various equipment and devices without compromising on the existing features and space. It is only practically achievable when the design, fabrication and installation of the customized features have been completed in concurrence with the manufacturing of the vehicle itself. Adaptive customization in vehicle design, on the other hand, can be implemented during or at any stage after the vehicle is manufactured and operational. However, to achieve effective and efficient ergonomic usage is a complex exercise. Mechanical possibilities and constraints, inherent in the vehicle, determine the customization quality, resulting in adaptive design solutions which may vary from a crude add-on to a neatly hidden solution.

General characteristics	Aim/context		How to design customized solutions to facilitate an optimal user experience when operating on-board computer and handling other equipment	
	Publication		Liem, André, "An ergonomic case study on the interior customisation of fast response cars based on vehicle adaptation", *International Journal of Vehicle Design*, Vol. 55, nos. 2–4, 2011.	
Organization of the project	Duration of project		June 2002–January 2003 (9 months)	
	Actors/stakeholders		– Singapore Police Force (SPF) – National University of Singapore (NUS) – Global Precision Engineering Pvt. Ltd.	
Dimensions of analysis	Orientation	Positioning	Domain	Product ergonomics
			Specialization	Physical
			Intervention	Preventive Erg. – Industrial Design
		Worldview	Constructivist	
		Generic Strategy	Systemic (in terms of design) Evolutionary (in terms of development of entire project)	
	Design reasoning model and method		Hermeneutic and reflective practice	
	Practice		Ergonomic and industrial design	
	Value creation		Cost saving, user experience, operations effectiveness	

In this preventive ergonomic design project, adaptative customization has been chosen as an orientation to enhance the interaction among the electronic communication devices, co-passenger and driver (Figure 5.10), as well as to facilitate the retrieval and storage of equipment and tools in the rear interior (Figure 5.12). A constructivist worldview aligned with systemic ways of strategizing has been adopted in the design of the interior. Prior to the commencement of the project no structured design methodology was proposed. Instead, a reflective practice-oriented approach was adopted in the conceptualization and detail design of the interior customization. Foam and cardboard models (see Figure 5.11) were used to obtain better knowledge on how the electronics, equipment and tools need to be arranged in a constrained space with respect to the user. This technique provides sufficient flexibility in the exploration of concepts and the performance of user trials [STA 98].

Figure 5.10. *Interacting with electronic on-board communication equipment in the front interior of the vehicle*

Figure 5.11. *Foam models to explore the positioning of equipment in the front and rear interior of the vehicles*

The final outcome showed that both design solutions for the Volvo and Mitsubishi have complied well with the ergonomic and on-the-road driving requirements, set by the SPF. However, the Mitsubishi performed better than the Volvo, as the spacious rear interior of the first provided a more ideal situation for retrieving and storing equipment. Regarding the workspace in the front of the vehicles, no significant differences have been observed in terms of interactions among driver, co-passenger and equipment.

The systemic nature of this project had an influence on the cost and value of the end product. The SPF purchased the electronic on-board equipment without consulting and negotiating with Volvo and Mitsubishi. This has led to a situation where both car manufacturers refused to undertake an integrative customization exercise, mainly because of responsibility issues. To highlight this responsibility issue, *"Who will be responsible if the electronic equipment does not function or the vehicle itself encounters complications? Is it the car manufacturer, SPF, the people who install the equipment, or the suppliers of the electronic equipment?"* In this case, the SPF was referred to independent subcontractors and designers for the customization project. This project is a clear example where the main actor (SPF) took an evolutionary approach, without considering the collaborative contexts of the stakeholders

Figure 5.12. *Retrieval of equipment form rear-interior of Mitsubishi and Volvo*

5.3.5. *Rucksack bag design to facilitate optimum loading (RBD Karrimor)*

Through a collaboration between Robert Feeney Associates (RFA) and Loughborough University of Technology, a rucksack bag for long distance hikers was designed for Karrimor International. Since the harness was already completed, the focus was on how to facilitate optimum loading and unloading of items. Accessibility, space optimization, comfort, stability and maneuverability and applicability in different contexts were key issues to be considered. The result was an integrated solution of a main backpack and a daypack. During long distance traveling, both packs merge into a uniformed holistic form. In a situation, when the traveller has found him- or herself a base accommodation and intends to make day trips, the daypack can then be used separately.

General characteristics	Problem/context		How to design a rucksack bag which facilitates optimal loading and distribution of weight while on the move.	
	Publication		Liem, André, "Rucksack bag design to facilitate optimum loading", Master's Thesis, 1994.	
Organization of the project	Duration of project		October 1993–June 1994	
	Actors/stakeholders		– Karrimor International Pvt. Ltd.	
			– Loughborough University of Technology (LUT)	
			– Robert Feeney Associates (RFA), Ergonomic and Design Consultants	
			– Delft University of Technology, Faculty of Industrial Design Engineering (TUD-ID)	
Dimensions of analysis	Orientation	Positioning	Domain	Product ergonomics
			Specialization	Physical
			Intervention	Preventive Erg. – Industrial Design
		Worldview	Positivist	
		Generic strategy	Systemic	
	Design reasoning model and method		Problem solving and participative	
	Practice		Ergonomic research and industrial design	
	Value creation		Profit making and user experience	

To achieve optimal comfort and performance, anthropometric experiments were conducted with respect to loads carrying under fixed laboratory and in-field conditions. The orientation of this industrial design project was based on a preventive intervention within the domain and specialization of physical product ergonomics. The emphasis on research indicated the positivistic nature of this project. A structured design approach was adopted to craft the problem definition and design requirements, as well as prescriptively suggest optimal ways of how to pack a backpack in a systemic context. Formal anthropometric and interview methods were used to gain new knowledge about loading, load distribution and load carrying, which were adopted to a certain extent, interviewed users were more involved than was expected and participated by giving concrete design suggestions.

In term of practice, this project showed how a designer dealt with a well-defined project brief, experimentation, testing and the management of quantitative data as a resource for hands on designing. Valuewise, additional profit for Karrimor International was pursued through continued research and project work in user experience design by Loughborough University and RFA.

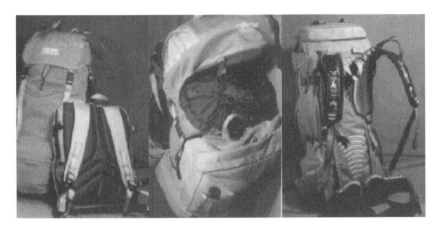

Figure 5.13. *Rucksack bag design to facilitate optimum loading*

5.4. Analysis of cases within prospective ergonomic intervention

In this section, the following cases will be discussed within the context of prospective ergonomic intervention:

– product planning versus product positioning;

– monitoring fish health;

– development of culture-driven design concepts;

– CAD as an idea and concept generation tool in the early design stages.

5.4.1. *Product planning versus product positioning (PP versus PP)*

General Characteristics	Problem/context		What method is most suitable in the search for innovative products and services?	
	Publication		Liem, André; Sanders, E.B.N, "Human-centred design workshops in collaborative strategic design projects; an educational and professional comparison", Design and Technology Education: an International Journal, vol. 18, no. 1, 2013.	
Organization of the project	Duration of project		August 2010–November 2010 (4 months)	
	Actors/stakeholders		Various Norwegian companies	
			Norwegian University of Science and Technology	
Dimensions of analysis	Orientation	Positioning	Domain	Product ergonomics
			Specialization	Physical, cognitive, organizational
			Intervention	Prospective – strategic design
		Worldview	Positivist	
		Generic strategy	Classical/systemic	
	Design reasoning model and method		Problem solving and participative	
	Practice		Strategic and industrial design	
	Value creation		Profit, user experience, business eco-system	

From 2005 to 2013, 8–10 established Norwegian firms were annually involved in a four-year collaborative strategic design project. The strategic design project was divided into two stages: product planning and management and industrial design. In groups of two or three, students were required to mimic design consultants.

In recent years, an alternative route to goal finding leading to more detailed directives in formulating the design brief was suggested through the implementation of product/service positioning maps for determining "value creation" opportunities [CAG 02]. The "how to" design was introduced as a response complementary to the "what to" design as framed by Ansoff's product-market-technology model [ANS 68]. The analysis of nine recent strategic design projects showed that visionary capabilities were important in generating radical and incremental innovations. As shown in Figure 5.14, a "new product–existing market" strategy was targeted in five of the nine projects, whereas two projects focused on creating a "new market for existing products and technologies". Two other companies embarked on a "natural" diversification strategy, because they were contract manufacturers and did not have any background and expertise in developing their own core products. Design goals were determined through discussions among company management and design students, driven by a conjecture–analytical design approach. When adopting Cagan and Vogel's positioning map, all low and high technology projects were categorized in the high style (ergonomics and form) quadrants (Figure 30B).

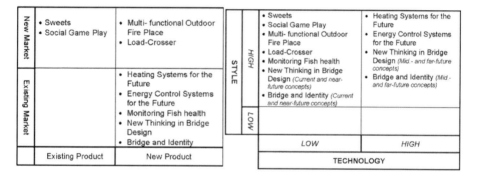

Figure 5.14. *a) Positioning of strategic design projects on product-market matrix; b) Positioning of strategic design projects on Cagan and Vogel's positioning map (2002)*

In terms of orientation, students were subjected to a product planning and management process, where they had to follow a systematic innovation-step model that guided them to determine their design brief [BUI 87, BUI 96]. The deliverables were innovative products and services. This project was driven by prospective intervention, which is dependent on the type of company collaboration, required physical, cognitive and/or organizational ergonomic specialization. Based on a positivistic worldview, the project aligns with a classical or systemic strategy, dependent on the contextual influence within each type of collaboration.

Concerning methods and practices, a structured problem-solving approach throughout the product planning and industrial stages was complemented by participative design interventions. The purpose of these interventions was to boost divergent creative thinking, find focus, as well as to align interests among stakeholders. Moreover, it can be clearly seen that prescribed methods are applicable to determine the innovative content of design projects, either from a "what" or "how" approach in both positioning frameworks. Hereby, social, economic and technological trends formed the basis for strategic thinking and innovation.

The value of using product planning and product positioning methods lies within the positivistic realm, mainly focusing on the fulfillment of economic needs. While taking into consideration user, organization and business ecosystem levels of involvement, the educational relevance of using these frameworks is to make students understand how to develop a structured business context for their project on which they can build further upon to be more specific in their goal product planning and designing activities.

5.4.2. *Monitoring fish health project (Fish Health)*

General characteristics	Problem/context		What are the methods and tools for monitoring fish health within fish farming activities?	
	Publication		Liem, André; Sanders, E.B.N., "Human-centred design workshops in collaborative strategic design projects; an educational and professional comparison", Design and Technology Education: an International Journal, vol. 18, no. 1, 2013.	
Organization of the project	Duration of project		August 2010–November 2010 (4 months)	
	Actors/stakeholders		– Norwegian fish framing companies – Telcage AS – Norwegian University of Science and Technology	
Dimensions of analysis	Orientation	Positioning	Domain	Product (service) ergonomics
			Specialization	Cognitive, organizational
			Intervention	Prospective – strategic design
		Worldview	Positivist	
		Generic strategy	Systemic	
	Design reasoning model and method		Problem solving and participative	
	Practice		Strategic and industrial design	
	Value creation		Profit making, User experience, network building	

Cocreation workshops focused on the context of "Sea-based Fish-farming", where students addressed problems and solutions related to monitoring fish health for an information service provider. The objective was to reveal interesting problem areas and business opportunities for the company and its stakeholders and to encourage these participants to be creative and generate new ideas. The company was a service provider, developing information and communication services (including the needed communication infrastructure) for the off-shore fish-farming market. Services were given on a subscription basis. Since the benefits of the services were not fully understood by the market (i.e., the market is "under developed"), it has been important for the service provider to develop the services in close co-operation with the users and other stakeholders.

The first workshop with "consumers" revealed existing knowledge and concerns around fish health related to the fish farming industry. The second workshop focused on idea generation and contextualization of roles and responsibilities, especially those of the service provider (Figure 5.15).

Figure 5.15. *Workshop with "stakeholders" revealing existing knowledge and concerns around fish health*

Ideas that emerged from the sessions were clustered into five categories. These were technical solutions, user-friendliness in surveillance, preventive and curative health care using telemedicine, documentation and facilitation of purchase through information. The conclusion from the idea development exercise was to make it easier for the fish farmers and veterinarians to detect illnesses early and decrease the damage, as well as to avoid financial losses connected to massive fish health problems.

In the third workshop, as new technologies (sensors, communication technology etc.) and new ways of working were introduced, needs and wishes of the different stakeholders connected to activities around fish health were further explored, which led to new opportunities discovered attached to fish health.

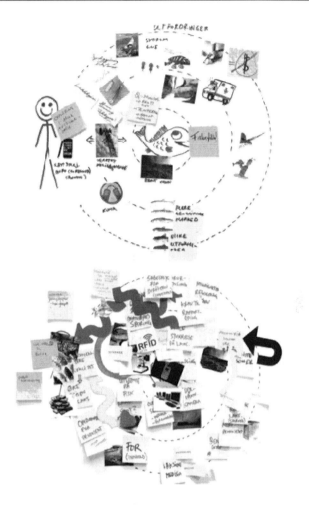

Figure 5.16. *Use of cocreation tools and methods to map out the context and generate ideas*

This project is predominantly service oriented. Ergonomic focus was on cognition and organization, as solutions were predicted to be in the field of user-interface design. Since the market is underdeveloped but the context clearly defined, a participative, structured problem solving approach has been practiced in the form of consecutive workshops as described above. Hereby the designer(s) acted as (a) facilitator(s) and introduced cocreation methods and tools to the various workshop participants. This approach aligns with a systemic generic strategy. From a value creation perspective, the workshops have provided useful insights for idea and concept generation in terms of technology implementation, content and service provision for a fish health surveillance interface. Through these insights, two main developments were ascertained:

– the usability and accessibility of the interface have improved through complementary services;

– technology development has led to increased information flow among stakeholders and complementary services.

5.4.3. *Development of culture-driven design concepts (Culture DCC)*

General Characteristics	Problem/context	How to propose and strategize innovate product and service concepts from an acculturation perspective?		
	Publication	Liem, André; Lind, Ane Linea; Gadaria, Dharmesh, "Towards a Culturally Driven Approach for the Development of Strategic Design Concepts", I: Proceedings of Norddesign: International Conference on Methods and Tools for Product and Production Development, Gothenburg, Sweden. The Design Society, pp. 97–108, 2010.		
Organization of the project	Duration of project	August 2009–December 2009 (5 Months)		
	Actors/stakeholders	Norwegian University of Science and Technology, Department of Product Design		
Dimensions of analysis	Orientation	Positioning	Domain	Product (service) ergonomics
			Specialization	Physical, cognitive, organizational
			Intervention	Prospective – strategic design
		Worldview	Constructivist	
		Generic strategy	Systemic	
	Design reasoning model and method		Hermeneutic, reflective practice	
	Practice		Strategic and industrial design	
	Value creation		Profit making, user experience, resource database	

This project proposed acculturation theories for designers to undertake a more comprehensive external analysis in the product planning stages of the innovation process. The concept was based on the assumption that extreme trends and developments in societies' political, economical and social situation are usually not favorable, and therefore perceived as a motivator for initiating incremental or radical product/service ideas. Several case studies have illustrated the difficulties in changing social, political and economical developments overnight in a society, and demonstrated the potential role of design in improving these difficulties through innovative design concepts. A bottom-up analysis of cases resulted in six preliminary categories, and function as a guide for a broader and more reflective approach in product planning and goal finding. These categories are as follows:

– healthcare and elderly care;

– working and living;

– education and manpower development;

– purchase of food, products and services;

– mobility/transportation of goods and people;

– interaction and communication.

This shows that a cultural approach toward external analysis and product idea generation in the front-end of innovation (FEI) can be instrumental in the generation of innovative system and or product ideas to improve quality of life and service not only in developing but also developed nations.

In terms of orientation, the diversity of case studies has demonstrated that a systemic approach based on culture and context toward strategic design should be further explored in the construction of *prospective* product service systems in the FEI. From a reflective and hermeneutic design reasoning perspective, these various case studies have illustrated the potential role of design in improving the negative aspects of these developments by understanding extreme cultural trends as well as the potential for acculturation. Potential *domains* for innovation are within the realm of product/service ergonomics with *specializations* either in physical, cognitive and/or organizational ergonomics.

With respect to method and practice, mapping case studies on a bipolar scale, which illustrates extreme cultural trends and developments in certain societies, facilitates the search for new product ideas in the FEI. Furthermore, the results of these mapping exercises can be consolidated into a resource of diverse cases, which help to bottom-up craft out a database of cases for product planning and goal finding. This database of cases, which is a valuable asset, needs to be refined and updated from time to time to maintain relevance as a source for external analysis in the generation of innovative system/product ideas.

5.4.4. *CAD as an idea and concept generation tool in the early design stages (CAD Tool)*

General characteristics	Aim/context	How to use CAD as an idea and concept generation tool in the development of new products?	
	Publication	Liem, André, "Computer aided design as an idea and concept generation tool in the early stages of the design process", *Proceedings of The Ninth Norddesign Conference, 2012,* The Design Society. 2012, 2012.	
Organization of the project	Duration of project	January 2012–May 2012 (5 Months)	
	Actors/stakeholders	Norwegian University of Science and Technology, Department of Product Design	
Dimensions of analysis	Orientation — Positioning	Domain	Product ergonomics
		Specialization	Physical, cognitive
		Intervention	Prospective – strategic design
	Orientation — Worldview	Positivist followed by a Constructivist	
	Generic Strategy	Systemic	
	Design reasoning model and method	Hermeneutic, reflective	
	Practice	Strategic and industrial design	
	Value creation	Cost reduction in design development, user experience, stakeholder involvement	

The existing tension field on *When, Where* and *How* to use conventional design representations versus CAD is becoming more and more prevalent. This research project attempted to argue that in certain circumstances digital visual representations (CAD) are more effective in the early creative idea and concept generation stages of the design process compared to sketches and drawings. In other words, intensive reflective and processual visualization activities, which immediately render feedback in computer media, encourage the designer to generate images more frequently and more precisely in his/her mind, compared to conventional media.

The above phenomenon has led to discussions around two factors, which redefine the value of CAD in an educational context. These factors are as follows:

– type of students admitted according to academic inclination;

– type of design program.

Results have shown that because of their sound academic abilities, students, who were admitted only upon good grades, demonstrated a strong aptitude toward learning different CAD systems. However, they were generally weak in (manual) sketching and drawing. This is explicitly shown in interactions among educators and students in the early stages of the idea development and concept generation stages where crucial stages of exploration and reflection are visualized by surprisingly well-developed CAD drawings/models, rather than manual sketches and drawings.

An interesting correlation can be seen between the type of design program and evangelized processes and methods. Industrial design engineering programs, who advocate a structured problem solving process and methods, based on analysis–synthesis, are very much inclined to promote CAD as early as possible in design and materialization activities. The inherent tension between CAD and conventional sketching, which is caused by the different perspectives on "what design is about", should encourage design programs to rethink and re-evaluate their educational objectives, in conjunction with which design tools are to be emphasized or not, in terms of design knowledge and skills transfer.

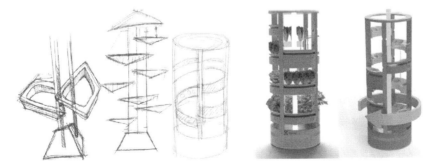

Figure 5.17. *Example of a design submission, where the student demonstrated poor manual representation, but good CAD modeling skills*

In terms of orientation, a positivistic worldview was initially adopted, where students, who participated in the Electrolux Design Lab 2012 competition, argued for the existence of a problem and attempted to solve it from a contextual and systemic viewpoint, based upon the theme, "design experience". In conjunction with the theme, a specific context was explored, researched and analyzed from Social, Technological, Economic, Environmental and Political (STEEP) perspectives. Most students were able to formulate clear consumer insights using a structured problem solving approach. However, methodologically and practice wise, students turned to a reflective mode of thinking. Instead of demonstrating design flair through the comprehensive and explicit representation of ideas and concepts, they developed ideas and initial concepts inwardly through low-quality thumbnail sketches and much verbal explanations. When the design concept became more concrete in their minds, these students quickly readopt a structured problem solving approach by extensively using digital design tools in the conceptualization, detailing and materialization stages.

The value of using CAD in the early design stages may lead to cost reduction in the design process through new ways of visually representing designs convincingly accurately and fast. Furthermore, the earlier CAD is adopted, the earlier stakeholders can be invited to participate in the design process.

6

Cross-Comparison of Cases

6.1. Introduction

The exchange of goods and services are becoming more intricate because of advanced technologies, complex user demands and stakeholder interactions. This requires design projects to be more context-driven with varied interests due to the (personal) ambitions and limitations of the different stakeholders. This phenomenon indicates that contextual issues and pluralistic objectives dictate the planning and implementation of the respective projects, emphasizing the importance of prospective ergonomic intervention in strategic or systems design projects. Positivist and constructivist worldviews have been adopted in these context-driven projects, supported by problem solving, hermeneutic, participative and reflective modes of design reasoning to anticipate future plural needs and objectives within the systemic quadrant. These plural needs and objectives within the context of business management and design comprise a balance among profit maximization, increased usability, work efficiency and effectiveness, human well-being, etc.

In the first stage of the analysis, cases will be cross-compared within each quadrant of the generic strategy framework [WHI 01]. Comparisons will be made according to the following criteria:

– positioning (domain, specialization, intervention);

– worldview;

– design reasoning mode and method;

– practice and stakeholder involvement;

– value creation.

In the second analysis stage, cases will be compared across the different quadrants, based on how each case is classified according to ergonomic and design intervention as well as how they are being mapped alongside the axes of "process" and "outcome" (see Figure 6.2). Figure 6.1 recaps and color codes the different projects according to ergonomic interventions. Besides that, it also highlights the domain and specialization of each project.

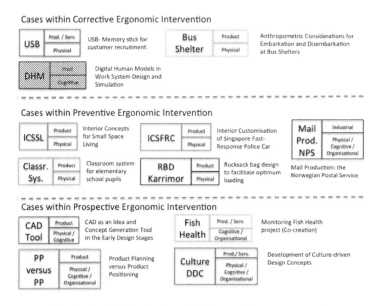

Figure 6.1. *Projects classified according to ergonomic intervention with their domains and specializations*

6.2. Cross-comparison of cases within the context of deliberate/planned processes and targeted outcomes profit maximization/problem solving

In this section, selected cases will be compared within the context of deliberate/planned processes and targeted outcomes pertaining to profit maximization and problem solving. Table 6.1 shows the cross-comparison from a classical strategy perspective.

In all these projects, a positivist worldview has been adopted because of the use of prescriptive and structured methods and processes to achieve strategic service or design results. Ergonomic intervention is mainly corrective and preventive because the contexts have been predetermined for the projects reported in the case studies. This also implies a problem-solving approach as a way to reason about design.

PE, which has been advocated in the "product planning and positioning" case, is strategic and builds upon prescriptive methods and tools. These prescriptive methods and tools have been used to determine the innovative content of educational and real-life projects, either from a "what to design" or "how to design" approach. For example, Ansoff's PMT-matrix and Cagan and Vogel's positioning maps were frequently used to classify and frame the objectives of the different collaborative projects. However, in terms of design reasoning, this case also advocates participatory design beyond a problem-solving approach to discover hidden needs and anticipate future ones.

Using product planning and product positioning methods and tools contributes significantly to the value of strategic design and PE while taking into consideration user, organization and business ecosystem levels of involvement.

From a system and human-centered design approach, an abundance of collective processes and methods have been introduced to manage complexity and to involve different stakeholders in strategic design projects.

With respect to the NPS case, few difficulties were experienced in defining the system's outer boundaries because the logistic structure of the system was partly determined by the nature of the project. However, more difficulties were encountered when determining intermediate boundaries and interface connectivity between the elements of the system, concerning overlapping scenarios and products.

In the design of a downtown check-in work system, formal anthropometric and interview methods are still very relevant to develop new knowledge. Hereby, the use of digital human models was a suitable platform to facilitate knowledge creation, design activity and communication among a broader network of stakeholders, enhancing the business ecosystem.

Using a work system simulation, spatial relationships among virtual humans, check-in facilities and the workplace within an external environment can be easily manipulated.

In the embarkation and disembarkation project concerning bus shelters, research contributed to architects' and LTAs' insights into designing universally accessible facilities. From a positivist worldview, observations and interviews were mainly used to determine design guidelines.

Classical Strategy Perspective	Positioning			World view	Design reasoning mode and method	Practice and stakeholder involvement	Value Creation
	Domain	Specialisation	Intervention				
Anthropometric Considerations: Embarkation / Disembarkation at Bus Shelters	Product	Physical	Industrial Design / Corrective Ergonomics	Positivist	Problem Solving	Anthropo-metric Research for Design involving LTA and NUS-ARCH	Design insights and guidelines
Mail Production: The Norwegian Postal Service	Industrial	Physical Cognitive Organisational	Systems Design Preventive Ergonomics	Positivist	Problem Solving	Ergonomic Systems Design / Industrial Design involving NPS, NTNU, Inventas AS	Cost savings / profit enhancement. Improvement of industrial ergonomic processes
Product Planning versus Product Positioning	Product / Service	Physical / Cognitive	Strategic Design / Prospective Ergonomics	Positivist	Problem Solving / Participative	Various companies subjected to strategic and industrial design	Increased Profit, User experience, Business Eco-system
Digital Human Models in Work System Design and Simulation	Product	Cognitive	Industrial and Detail Design / Corrective Ergonomics	Positivist	Problem Solving	Ergonomic Research and Design involving MRT-Singapore and NUS-ARCH	Design guidelines. Enhancement of the business eco-system

Table 6.1. Cross-comparison of cases within the context of deliberate/planned processes and targeted outcomes of profit maximization/problem solving

6.3. Cross-comparison of cases within the context of emergent processes and targeted outcomes: profit maximization/problem solving

In this section, selected cases will be compared within the context of emergent processes and targeted outcomes pertaining to profit maximization and problem solving. Table 6.2 shows the cross-comparison between the projects and criteria.

In the adoption of an evolutionary strategy perspective, the two cases were characterized by a physical product or product-service offering. Although strategic design was emphasized in the USB project, the ergonomic intervention was corrective in nature. The constructivist/ pragmatic worldview dictates an evolutionary perspective, which does not propel the development of new products and services into the realm of PE.

Moreover, as design developments are emergent in nature, carefully planned processes and the use of structured methods have been absent in both cases. Instead, hermeneutic and reflective reasoning have taken center stage in design and development activities.

Stakeholders were actively involved in the design process but were not subject to participatory design methods. Value creation is short- and mid-term based and is determined by increased work efficiency, cost minimization and profit maximization. This is exemplified by the FRC project, where the Singapore Police Force has opted for adaptive instead of integrative customization of on-board equipment and interior design.

6.4. Cross-comparison of cases within the context of deliberate processes and pluralistic outcomes

In this section, selected cases will be compared within the context of deliberate processes and pluralistic outcomes. Table 6.3 shows the cross-comparison between the projects and criteria.

From a value creation perspective, profit making or cost saving is not the only objective in these systemic projects. User experience and developing networks with stakeholders are equally important if not more so. For example, in the rucksack bag project, structured research and design methods were adopted to systematically develop and suggest optimal ways of packing, considering the experience of different type of travelers, as well as the contexts they are traveling in.

Evolutionary Strategy Perspective	Positioning			Worldview	Design reasoning model and method	Practice and stakeholder involvement	Value Creation
	Domain	Specialisation	Intervention				
USB Memory Stick for Customer Recruitment	Product /Service	Physical	Strategic Design / Corrective Ergonomics	Constructivist / Pragmatic	Reflective / Practice / Participatory	Industrial and detail design involving UOB, Valen-Techn. and other stakeholders	Profit, Building and enlargement of customer base
Interior Customisation of Singapore Fast-Response Police Car	Product	Physical	Industrial Design Preventive Ergonomics	Constructivist	Hermeneutic / Reflective / Practice / Participative	Ergonomic and Industrial Design involving SPF, NUS-ARCH, and Global Prec. Eng.	Cost saving, User experience, Operations Effectiveness

Table 6.2. *Cross-comparison of cases within the context of emergent processes and targeted outcomes of profit maximization/problem solving*

Systemic Strategy Perspective	Positioning			Worldview	Design reasoning model and method	Practice and stakeholder involvement	Value Creation
	Domain	Specialisation	Intervention				
Classroom System for Elementary School Pupils	Product	Physical	Systems Design / Preventive Ergonomics	Positivist	Problem Solving, Hermeneutics, Reflective Practice	Ergonomic Systems Design and Industrial Design involving Moelven AS	Portfolio and profit enhancement. New insights in organising design studio teaching.
Interior Concepts for Small-space Living	Product	Physical	Systems Design / Preventive Ergonomics	Positivist	Problem Solving, Hermeneutics, Reflective Practice	Ergonomic Systems Design and Industrial Design involving HDB and NUS-ARCH	Happiness / Eco-Footprint
Rucksack Bag Design to Facilitate Optimum Loading	Product	Physical	Industrial Design / Preventive Ergonomics	Positivist	Problem Solving/ Participative	Ergonomic Research and Industrial Design involving Karrimor Int., LCT, TUD-ID and RFA.	Profit making, User experience
Product Planning versus Product Positioning	Product / Service	Physical / Cognitive	Strategic Design / Prospective Ergonomics	Positivist	Problem Solving / Participative	Various companies subjected to strategic and industrial design	Increased Profit, User experience, Business Eco-system
Monitoring Fish Health	Product / Service	Cognitive / organisational	Systems Design / Prospective Ergonomics	Positivist	Problem Solving / Participative	Strategic and Industrial Design involving Telcage and Norwegian fish farming companies	Profit making, User experience, Network building
Development of Culture-Driven Design Concepts	Product / Service	Physical Cognitive Organisational	Strategic Design / Prospective Ergonomics	Constructivist	Hermeneutics, Reflective Practice	Strategic and Industrial Design	Profit making, User experience, Resource database
CAD as an Idea and Concept Generation Tool in the Early Design Stages.	Product	Physical Cognitive	Strategic Design / Prospective Ergonomics	Positivist / Constructivist	Hermeneutics, Reflective Practice	Strategic and Industrial Design involving Electrolux Design Lab	Cost reduction in design / development User experience. Stakeholder involvement

Table 6.3. *Cross-comparison of cases within the context of deliberate processes and targeted outcomes of profit maximization/problem solving*

The above example illustrates that cases, which are situated in specific contexts, require to a certain extend planned and structured processes as well as prescriptive methods to determine the outcome of the project.

This justifies that a positivist worldview is central in systemic cases, which is characterized by extensive stakeholder participation.

Concerning the prospective ergonomic/strategic design interventions, participative and problem solving reasoning modes were prevalent if the design project suggests a democratic participation of their stakeholders. If the design project is very much influenced by the views and opinions of the designer, pluralistic outcomes are being reached by hermeneutic or reflective practice modes of design reasoning.

An example of a democratic case is the "Fish-Health Monitoring" project. The co-creation workshops focused on the context of "sea-based fish-farming", where students addressed problems and solutions related to monitoring fish health for an information service provider.

Using a toolkit, the primary objective of the participatory workshop sessions was to reveal interesting problem areas and business opportunities for a fish health surveillance interface for the company and its stakeholders, as well as to encourage these participants to co-create new ideas in terms of technology implementation, content and service provision.

Cases that deviate fully or partly from deliberate and prescriptive ways of research and design are (1) the development of culture-driven design concepts and (2) CAD as an idea and concept generation tool in the early design stages.

In the "Culture-Drive-Design Concepts" case, extreme cultural and behavioral trends and developments in nations' social, technological, economical, environmental and political situations, positioned on a bipolar spectrum, were instigators for strategic and innovative product and service planning. A cultural understanding of societies and regions supported these trends and developments.

This methodology, which is constructivist in nature, requires a diverse database of cases to be developed. Moreover, cases are to be refined and categorized from time to time based on typical contexts and events. Furthermore, to be prescriptively applied as a source for external analysis in the generation of innovative system/product ideas, characteristics of case studies need to be structured and formalized.

To exemplify the value of a cultural approach, a systematic and context-based design process has been applied in the "Classroom Systems" and "Interior Concept for Small Space Living" projects. In these projects, hermeneutic and reflective practice modes complement a problem-solving approach. Hereby, the way a system should look is very much influenced by how the designer interprets and translates the formation of a specific context into a holistic system of interacting elements. However, as the ergonomic intervention is preventive, the immediate environment and stakeholders determine the aims of the project and their system constraints.

In the CAD and Idea/Concept Generation Tool case, the debate is how to balance the development of practical skills and thinking aptitudes. Participation in the Electrolux Design Lab competition has revealed that students, who were admitted only upon good grades, were generally poor in (manual) sketching and drawing. However, due to their solid academic capabilities, they were capable of envisioning future needs and effectively mastering different CAD systems in a short period of time. This proves that students were able to practice design thinking from different modes of design reasoning; a hermeneutic and constructivist mode in terms of idea generation and goal finding, as well as a structured problem solving mode in learning and using CAD in a versatile manner. Furthermore, the compilation of CAD and conventional representations in the early stages of the design process facilitated the involvement of other stakeholders in the network.

6.5. Comparison of case clusters across the four quadrants

Figure 6.2 gives an overview of how the different cases are positioned within a generic strategy map [WHI 01]. Most of the cases are positioned within the systemic and none in the processual quadrant. Cases characterized by a prospective ergonomic intervention are strategy- or systems-driven and mainly systemic in nature. This indicates that contextual issues and pluralistic objectives dictate the planning and implementation of the respective projects. Positivist and constructivist worldviews have been adopted in these projects, supported by problem solving, hermeneutic, participative and reflective modes of design reasoning. Expressed in a simplified manner, the exchange of goods and services are becoming more intricate because of advanced technologies, complex user demands and stakeholder interaction. This requires design projects to be more context-driven with varied interests due to the (personal) ambitions and limitations of the different stakeholders. What bind the projects together from a prospective and preventive ergonomic intervention are their aims to anticipate and satisfy future user experience. Projects, which are research-driven and where their design scope has been predetermined, are classified within the classical quadrant. Corrective and preventive ergonomic interventions aimed at, for example, solving a particular problem or maximizing profit were specific and required structured planning to achieve them. Hereby, the designer adopted a problem solving approach toward design based upon a positivist worldview. The product planning versus product positioning case is also positioned in the classical quadrant because some of the strategic design projects were accomplished using a prescriptive product planning and goal finding process.

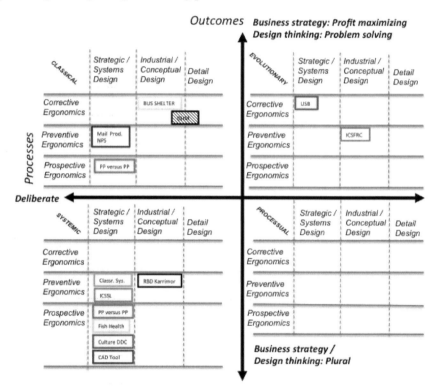

Figure 6.2. *An overview of the 12 cases positioned within a generic strategy map and characterized according to ergonomic and design intervention*

6.6. Qualitative analysis of cases according to intervention, worldviews, models of design reasoning and generic strategies

In this section, a qualitative assessment of the 12 cases will be presented. The assessment is based upon the juxtapositioning of the different ergonomic and design interventions with worldviews, models of design reasoning and generic strategies (see Table 6.4).

		Ergonomic intervention			Design intervention		
		Prospective ergonomics	Design ergonomics	Corrective ergonomics	Strategic/ systems design	Industrial design	Detail design
Worldview	Positivism	+	++	+	++	+	-
	Constructivism	+	-	-	+	-	–
	Pragmatism	–	–	-	-	–	–
	Advocacy	–	–	–	-	–	–
Models of design reasoning	Problem Solving	+	++	+	+++	-	-
	Hermeneutic	+	+	–	++	-	–
	Reflective	+	+	-	++	-	–
	Participative	+	-	–	+	–	–
	Normative	–	–	–	–	–	–
	Social	–	–	–	–	–	–
Generic strategies	Classical	-	-	+	+	+	–
	Evolutionary	–	–	–	–	-	–
	Processual	–	–	–	–	–	–
	Systemic	++	++	–	++	+	–

Table 6.4. *Ergonomic and design interventions juxtaposed against worldviews, models of design reasoning and generic strategies*

Since most of the cases carry two or more perspectives on the type of intervention, worldview, mode of design reasoning and strategy, a qualitative approach has been used to analyze trends rather than to specifically pinpoint qualitative results.

Prospective ergonomic intervention happened in only four out of the 12 projects, which were positivist and/or constructivist in nature. Positivist because planned processes have been used but constructivist because outcomes, due to contextual reasons and bounded rationality, are plural. This undoubtedly implies that the wide range of design reasoning models from problem solving to participative design are suited to be used with each other. On a management level, the dualistic nature of these cases, which in some instances are positivistic and in other instances are constructivist, aligns well with a systemic generic strategy.

An example of such a case is the "CAD as an Idea and Concept Generation Tool in the Early Design Stages". Although CAD has extensively been used as a tool in the generation of detailed concepts for the Electrolux Design competition by most of the participants, the thinking behind the concepts is mostly hermeneutic and reflective in nature. However, this case can be classified as systemic because the themes and deliverables for the competition are predefined and the outcomes are plural: cost reduction in design/development, enhanced user experience and stakeholder involvement.

Similarly, cases where strategic or systems intervention took place were mostly positivistic and constructivist in nature. In these strategic/systems design cases, problem solving, reflective and hermeneutic modes of reasoning have been adopted to develop design solutions, mostly tied to specific contexts. This signifies that a majority of the strategic- and systems-intervened design cases are also systemic in nature but driven by context rather than bounded by human rationality.

Moreover, a combination of preventive ergonomic and systems design intervention was present in the following cases:

– mail production at the Norwegian Postal Service;

– classroom systems for elementary school pupils;

– the interior concepts for small-space living project.

In each of these cases, a design brief has been presented at systems level. The scope of the projects determined the boundaries of the system.

There are some similarities between cases which were subjected to industrial design and preventive ergonomic intervention. Mainly, a positivist worldview has been adopted in the development of design solutions. Complementary to a problem solving mode of reasoning, elements of reflective and hermeneutic thinking were present. These cases, which encapsulated a preventive ergonomic and industrial design intervention, also aligned well with a systemic view of strategizing because the design briefs determine their design space, limitations and possibilities.

A typical example, which embodies a preventive ergonomic and industrial design intervention, is the "Interior Customisation of Singapore Fast-Response Police Car". However, in this typical case, the project is constructivist in nature and very much driven by a hermeneutic, reflective practice and participatory modes of design reasoning. From an evolutionary strategy perspective, cost savings, operational effectiveness and enhanced user experiences are values which have been targeted.

For cases, which have been intervened from a corrective ergonomic perspective, a positivistic/pragmatic worldview complemented by problem solving and reflective modes of reasoning has been adopted. Related generic strategies are mainly classical and evolutionary because these cases are aimed at "concrete business and design objectives" through redesign.

The case "Digital Human Models in Work System Design and Simulation" shows how corrective ergonomic and partly detail design interventions have been applied in developing design guidelines for baggage check-in at mass rapid transit stations in Singapore.

Two cases were positioned in the evolutionary quadrant. In these cases, the designer used an emergent constructivist and pragmatic approach to meet the design goals. Reflective reasoning with the business context was an important impetus for taking an opportunistic design and development approach in the USB project and a trial and error approach in the customization of the Singapore police car interior.

Figure 6.3 complements Figure 6.2 by showing how the 12 cases are positioned according to worldview and design reasoning mode. Although no direct correlations can be made with types of interventions and generic strategy positioning, it can be said that most projects were positivistic in nature and were subjected to a diversity of design reasoning approaches to achieve conceptual or tangible results. However, a group of projects were characterized as constructivist and pragmatic. Designers adopted foremost a reflective practice and hermeneutic approach in formulating the final design brief or in creating a materialized design solution.

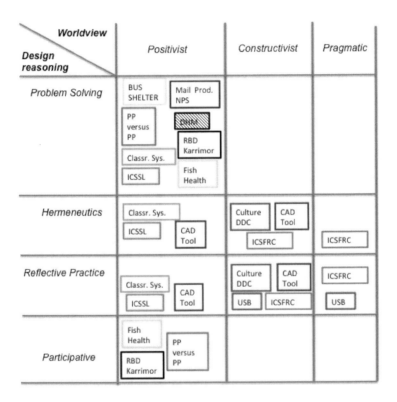

Figure 6.3. *An overview of the 12 cases positioned according to worldview and design reasoning mode*

When adopting a prospective ergonomic view, only the "culture DDC" project was constructivist in nature, where hermeneutic and reflective reasoning prevailed. This shows that PE interventions foremost rely on prescriptive processes, methods and tools.

To conclude this chapter, 12 cases have been mapped according to ergonomic and design intervention. Figure 6.4 provides a summarized overview of the relationship between ergonomic and design interventions.

The mapping exercise has shown that PE as well as strategic/systems intervention took place in four out of 12 cases. Four projects were broadly defined with no clear system boundaries of the product or service. Three out of the 12 were the result of strategic/systems design and preventive ergonomic intervention. In these three cases, the project brief and system boundaries have been clearly predetermined. A preventive ergonomic intervention has mainly been adopted in the creation of system elements (products). An exceptional case is the USB project. The business case is strategic in nature but the design of the product, which embodies the business intent, is a redesign of existing USBs. In two out of 12 cases, straightforward industrial design and preventive ergonomic intervention led to novel design outputs which have never been referenced to previous designs before.

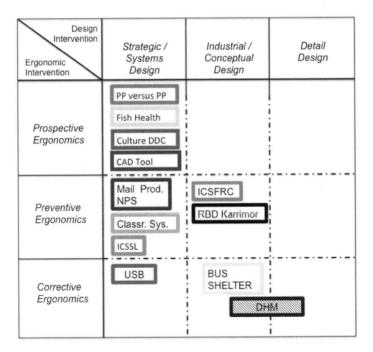

Figure 6.4. *Twelve cases positioned and juxtaposed according to ergonomic and design intervention*

The "Bus shelter" and "DHM" case are industrial design projects with a tendency to be more detail design oriented. In both cases, the scope of ergonomic intervention has been narrowly defined. In the "Bus shelter project", it is about investigating and solving the embarkation/disembarkation gap, while in the DHM acceptable queuing standards based upon body ellipse theories has been investigated. Given this predefined and rather narrow context, these cases are characterized as "corrective ergonomic" interventions.

On a final note, prospective and preventive ergonomic interventions alongside strategic and systems design interventions are prevalent in a majority of the cases (seven out of 12). Both interventions adopt a human-centered approach in the design and development of innovative products and concepts, focusing on increased usability, work efficiency and effectiveness and human well-being. The main difference between a preventive and prospective ergonomic intervention in strategic design projects is that the former accepts a given context or brief while the latter redefines them, as well as their outcomes, and how to achieve these outcomes.

7

Discussion

7.1. Introduction

From an educational standpoint, students and novice designers may not always easily comprehend the shift from a theoretical to a practice-based approach in design, and often lack the experience of practice in order to develop contextual and holistic understandings of what they have been taught. To bridge this gap between design theory and practice, it is necessary to develop prospective ergonomic (PE) mindsets among academics and practicing designers through modes of reasoning, methods and tools as social sustainability and service-oriented design thinking are becoming more important for developing innovative products and experiences. This implies that they should be engaged more frequently in mentorship and scholarship activities through collaboration with the industry, involving a broader network of stakeholders and targeting different levels of value innovation.

In this chapter, the earlier mentioned research questions will be discussed with respect to how innovation driven PEs can be contextualized and reframed within overarching and subordinate fields of ergonomics and distinguished from strategic design and management.

Hereby, orientation, methods, practices and value are the criteria which will be used for discussing the similarities and differences between macroergonomics and strategic management, PE and strategic design, preventive ergonomics and industrial design, corrective ergonomics and detail design.

Finally, this chapter will conclude with a general discussion on PE and its relation to strategic design and strategic management with respect to the development of new products and services.

7.2. Orientation

In this work, differences and similarities between PE and strategic design have been discussed with reference to generic strategies based upon innovation attitudes and ambitions within and among an ecosystem of organizations and stakeholders.

With respect to the motivations for developing future products and services, it can be said that in strategic design, innovation is centered around the growth and development of the organization, whereas in PE a balance between performance/productivity on the one hand and human well-being on the other is sought after.

However, a common perspective established between strategic design and PE is the aim to develop new products and services by imagining future user needs and responding with creative design solutions in a Fuzzy–Front End of Innovation process. Compared to strategic design, where product planning activities also address incremental product extensions, PE mainly focuses on radical innovation centered on human well-being and interests. The clustering of PE projects with a strategic intent in Whittington's systemic quadrant of generic strategies is a proof of this (see Figure 6.4).

In industrial design and preventive ergonomic projects, context, the initial problem or brief are usually defined. Industrial design approaches the design problem through various perspectives: form, ergonomics, technology, marketing and ecology. However, in preventive ergonomics, user and usability aspects will be emphasized. Similarly, the comparison between industrial design and preventive ergonomics also applies when comparing detail design with corrective ergonomics.

7.3. Processes and methods

In strategic and industrial design projects, finding "what to develop" in the fuzzy-front-end is usually driven by the designer with the help of passive involvement of users and other stakeholders *(user-centered design)*. In this positivist, problem solving approach, structured processes and methods for product planning and goal finding are being applied. In PE, reflective and participatory methods and tools complement the structured and systematic processes, methods and tools for determining what to design and how to design it. The designer then acts as a facilitator who deliberately plans and manages co-creation sessions by orchestrating a compilation of design methods and tools to be directly applied and/or to be introduced in a participatory manner. He also constructively extracts stakeholders' views and competencies to anticipate and create future incremental or radical innovation based on user needs.

Concerning preventive ergonomic interventions, prescriptive analytical research and user-centered methods are being advocated to discover and understand user needs. Constrained by existing resources and contexts, the ergonomist creates new products or systems in a given context and according to a predetermined design brief. In some cases, such as in the ICSFRC project, a constructivist way of designing took place, in this case to design the interior of a fast-response car. Due to the highly contextual constraints, which are the predetermined interior spaces of the Mitsubishi and Volvo, on the spot model making and prototyping, sketching, and trial and fit sessions were the predominant activities, which signified a reflective design process. Corrective ergonomics intervened on strategic, industrial and detail design levels. Projects where corrective interventions lead to an industrial and detail design outcome were positivist in nature, driven by research and analysis. Examples are the Bus Shelter and DHM projects. The USB project, which is characterized by a strategic design – corrective ergonomic intervention – is evolutionary in nature. Since the design is a means to an end (the main objective is to enlarge the clientele for UOB's ladies' card), a reflective design approach has been chosen to opportunistically capitalize on unpatented technologies (electronics), as well as Valen Technologies' injection molding capabilities, in order to create low-cost USBs.

7.4. Practices

The difference between strategic design and PE with respect to practices is that the latter adopts a broader view toward stakeholders' interests. Reported PE cases incorporate a strategic intent and are positioned in the systemic quadrant. This means that although processes and methods are carefully planned, objectives and interests are more nuanced. Unlike in pure strategic design projects, where organizational interests and profitmaking are very much prioritized, PE acknowledges the individual interests and capabilities of different internal and external stakeholders at a microlevel. Furthermore, it acknowledges that these interests are pluralistic and different for each individual. In terms of innovation, the imagination and design of "human activities" through services, systems or products are being prioritized, sometimes in contrast to strategic design and management, where these are embedded in organizational aims.

For cases that are categorized under preventive or corrective ergonomics, the user is mainly considered as a passive actor in a design project. Furthermore, human activities are existing and observable.

7.5. Value creation

The nature of ergonomics, which focuses on human well-being, inherently promotes long-term profitability in organizations. The concept of achieving long-term profitability and at the same time human well-being can be achieved through socially responsible internal productivity measures within various units of the organization, for example by eliminating hazardous and occupationally unsound working processes, there may be lesser absenteeism, which leads to cost reduction.

When discussing value creation through innovation, PE is a field which facilitates the development of radically new products, systems and services, centered around the creation of human needs and improvement of human well-being. Hereby, an outward looking ergonomic perspective is being adopted in long-term profit making.

From a strategic management and design viewpoint, value can be achieved by focusing on long- and/or short-term profits. The outward looking perspective of strategic design, which aims at increased sales or innovative products and services, is being complemented by cost reduction when adopting a broader strategic management perspective toward profit maximization.

7.6. Implications for design education

Since design education is a topic which seeks coherence among the different cases, as outlined and discussed in Chapters 5 and 6, a pedagogical reflection will be made in this section on how to relate the teaching of strategic design and industrial design with different ergonomic interventions, especially PE. Furthermore, newly redefined paradigms in higher education (HE) and research, specifically mentorship, scholarship and service, will be discussed in terms of how they can contribute to the field of PE.

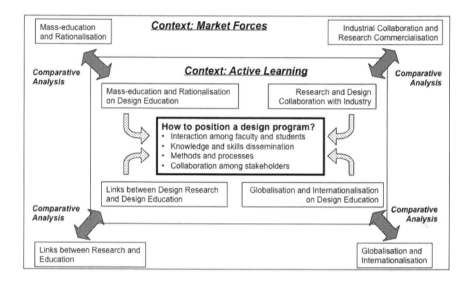

Figure 7.1. *Positioning design education within the context of "market forces" and "active learning" [LIE 14]*

From an overarching market perspective, four trends will be presented to provide a background for discussing how design programs are to be developed taking into consideration PE. These trends are as follows: (1) mass education and rationalization, (2) connections between education and research, (3) globalization and internationalization and (4) collaboration with industry and commercialization (see Figure 7.1 [LIE 14]).

7.6.1. *A PE intervention on mass education, rationalization and industrial design education*

The trend in societies where wealth is more equally distributed and education more accessible has fundamentally transformed the HE system to become more expansive and inclusive toward the mobility of students and scholars and movement of academic programs and institutions across borders [ALT 09].

However, counter-measuring the extraordinary impact of technology, and massification within HE, industrial design education still pursues distinct values and pedagogies that emphasize the importance of low student-faculty ratios, such as project-based learning, one-to-one tutorials, small group critiques and significant quantities of individual formative feedback and guidance [SWA 02, DES 06].

According to Yang *et al.* [YAN 05], these highly interactive student-faculty pedagogies may enhance the following three areas in terms of competency building:

– generic attributes, such as problem solving and communication skills, to rapidly react to immediate contextual changes;

– specific industrial design skills and knowledge, including design thinking, design methodology, graphical representation and communication, product development and manufacturing processes, manufacturing, materials, design management, environmental awareness and model making;

– ancillary skills, such as negotiation with clients [LEW 02], project management and communication [SIG 10].

This expansion of required competencies has enabled designers to play a more critical, integrative and active role in product development processes [SET 01]. For example, the 21st Century designer is expected to fulfill the roles of innovator, knowledge worker, sustainable entrepreneur and responsible citizen concerned with environmental, societal, commercial, communication issues and so on [PRE 03].

Furthermore, increasingly complex technologies coupled with more demanding consumers require specialized designing and design research competencies in order to anticipate user needs and introduce more user-friendly products or systems.

The need for competency management has been exemplified in the Norwegian Postal Service case (Section 5.3.1) In this project, students experienced few difficulties in defining the system's outer boundaries when the logistic structure of system was partly determined by the nature of the project. However, in the transition from group to individual work some problems were encountered in determining intermediate boundaries and interface connectivity between the elements of the system concerning overlapping scenarios and products. This calls for collective design processes and methods to better understand and clarify the roles of the stakeholders involved.

Being aware of the demanding and sometimes contradictory competency requirements, a PE approach toward mentorship and scholarship should be adopted, not only to improve the faculty's classroom but also to advance the practice beyond it, which means educating and preparing graduates for "managing" an ever-changing industrial and societal context [TRA 09].

7.6.2. A PE view on how to link research and education

According to the core values of classical European university education, which is embodied in the "Humboldt" model [BLO 05], there is no border between teaching and research. They are complementary and transient activities in knowledge creation and interpretation [WIL 91, KJE 10].

In the future, this means that "teaching", "research" and "administration" need to be redefined into, respectively, "mentorship", "scholarship" and "service", to be perceived as a more global and long-term commitment determined by *discovery, integration, application* and *knowledge transfer* [BOY 90, LIE 08]. Typically, this applies to the education of professional design practices where a mentoring relationship comprises more personal, closer relationships that demand time, commitment and a level of emotional engagement [BHA 00].

As a proposed learning concept which opposes traditional methods of classroom teaching, hierarchical and collaborative learning could be an avenue to promote an interactive way of customized learning and knowledge transfer in design. Hereby, a concept of "Vertical Studio Teaching and Learning" in conjunction with a system approach toward managing complex design and organizational problems has been proposed as one of the avenues to integrate industrial design better in an HE research environment.

Vertical studio teaching as an approach to coordinate systems design does not only elevate the designer's ability to manage complex design problems, but also addresses the intricacies of collaboration and social learning. When these complex design problems are managed thoroughly, it will create opportunities for students, practitioners, researchers and academics and other stakeholders within the same community of practice to collaborate more efficiently according to a master-apprenticeship model of learning.

The implementation of a structured hierarchical learning system, based on such a master-apprentice relationship throughout all levels of the "learning" organization, requires the intervention of PE, when managing complex strategic and systems design projects. For example, the focus in the interior classroom for the elementary school pupils project was on context-based system thinking. In the interactions among group members, teachers and collaborating companies, "reflective" [SCH 95] and "hermeneutic" [BAM 02, SNO 92, DAR 79] approaches to design thinking were used to complement a problem solving oriented way of designing. This reflective and hermeneutic way of designing enhanced by legitimate peripheral participation (LPP) modes of iterative learning [LAV 91] introduced elements of confusion but positively enhanced hierarchical and experiential learning [KOL 14].

7.6.3. *Globalization of HE*

Changing demands in HE, driven by European integration, global market forces and technological advancement, have pressured universities to compete by integrating the international dimension into their research and educational frameworks [END 04].

With respect to design and PE, globalization of HE may encourage web-based delivery of postgraduate courses. Based upon experiences with the Open University, the focus on information and communication technology (ICT) faculty teaching activities improved the satisfaction and motivation rate among students in their research and design projects [TJØ 10]. ICT platforms, mechanisms and delivery tools, such as Lynda [LYN 13] and MOOCS [WAL 13], facilitate physical studio space in face-to-face interactions, enabling flexible peer support, creativity and providing more platforms for various stakeholders in a virtual as well as physical comfort.

7.6.4. *Increased collaboration with industry and commercialization of research*

Due to on-going globalization trends, universities are expected to become an integral part of national or regional innovation endeavors. At this level, research-intensive universities are expected to be interactive players who collaborate closely with industry, the community and government [ETZ 97].

Filtering down to design education, students need to be adequately prepared on how to collaborate, negotiate and compromise when they engage themselves in university-industry collaborative design projects [NIE 01].

Moreover, if design aims to engage itself in the future university-education model, it needs to develop connections among subjects, people, disciplines and competencies, which implies facilitating participation and communication within a single organization, within business ecosystems, and among groups of (potential) users [BRA 04]. Furthermore, the emphasis on service design research has transitioned knowledge production from being mono- to cross-disciplinary, which opened up nonlinear and transient collaboration, expanding the number of research or knowledge actors [LAU 00].

From a PE perspective, the challenge is to sustain and extend a problem-solving attitude to anticipate future needs within a systemic strategy context. At the same time, yielding effective outcomes and meeting the economical interests of industrial collaborators should be driven by the use of effective methods for design development [FRI 00].

7.6.5. *The need for industrial design education and research to adapt to future developments in HE*

Since the introduction of a scientific design approach by the Ulm School, the traditional perception of the designer as a creative genius or stylist has changed significantly. Based on acquired "active" and "problem-based learning" skills and attitudes, he or she is currently seen as a team member, interpreter of complex systems, communicator and problem solver [ROT 99].

Moreover, as social sustainability and service-oriented design thinking are becoming more important for developing innovative products and experiences, students should be equipped with basic knowledge about different worldviews and design reasoning models [LIE 12] in order to be able to select the most appropriate processes and methods and to design with a PE mindset. They should be able to select the most suitable approaches, varying from structured processes such as "problem solving", "normative" and "social" to emergent practices such as "hermeneutics", "reflective practice" and "participatory".

From a professional practice perspective, it has been debated whether or not industrial design education should succumb to market-driven and massification trends imposed by HE take up the challenge to pursue one-to-one faculty-student relationships in "design studio" interactions [SCO 98]. However, this debate also underlines that if traditional design education is solely pursued, changes are inevitable. Assumed trust between master and apprentice needs to become more explicit and formal [TRA 09].

This means that orientations among faculty members toward research, teaching and administration need to be redefined as well as support structures redesigned to realize a PE-driven design program. Implications are as follows:

– faculty should be involved in mentorship and scholarship when advocating PE through learning and inquiry from a theoretical, collaborative and process perspective (research-based learning) [LIE 08]. Concretely, this implies the study of design processes, methods and behaviors contextualized within social, economic and cultural phenomena;

– practicing designers should be engaged more frequently in mentorship to contribute in skills development and sharing of design experiences through a hermeneutic "design thinking" and "designing" lens. These practicing designers can also act as a role model for students on how to plan and manage their projects, as well as how to act convincingly and persuasively in project management and negotiation situations;

– a team of dedicated faculty members and design practitioners should be established, who share consensus in promoting human-centered strategic design and innovation perspectives, processes and methods to imagine and generate new products and services;

– complementary to interdisciplinary teamwork in design projects and research [RIT 73], the concepts of "social learning" and LPP [BRO 89, WEN 00] should be introduced to students and novice designers to train them to work within complex collaborative contexts which are often bounded by rationality. In practice, this implies that those who are new to the community of design need to become acquainted with the tasks, vocabulary and organizing principles through peripheral activities first, before engaging in more complex senior level tasks and responsibilities [LAV 91, BRO 89];

– from a reflective practice perspective, experimentation, testing and quantitative evaluation of data should be inculcated among students when dealing with open-ended design problems. For example, CAD educators should encourage more explorative and reflective ways of tool use, rather than introducing them merely for presentation purposes;

– faculty should be engaged in mentorship and scholarship beyond the "physical home-based studio environment" through the use of media technologies for distance education.

7.7. General perspectives on PE and strategic design

The analysis of the 12 cases underlines that the development of innovative products and services is a common goal for strategic design and PE. However, there are some differences between them. Innovation within the context of strategic design is more about profit-making while PE seeks a balance between performance and productivity on the one hand and human welfare on the other. Compared to strategic design, where radical or incremental innovation is primarily driven by the intention of the designer with more or less passive involvement of users and other stakeholders, PE focuses on anticipating future needs in order to respond with creative design solutions. Even though these ideas are in their infancy stages, they take into account the systemic human, social, economical and technological constraints. In a synthetic way, this thesis puts forward five ideas:

1) strong relations exist between PE and strategic design which describe different viewpoints:

i) both fields share a common ground in "modern" strategic management/innovation;

ii) both fields support a deliberate way of "doing things", where planning is an important factor to achieve certain outcomes, whether specific/concrete or plural;

iii) the adoption of PE and strategic design processes are relevant for managing the early stages of development projects as well as for developing strategic directions.

2) PE embraces certain characteristics. For each case which has been analyzed and categorized as a typical case intervened through PE, we are able to conclude that:

i) PE promotes a system-oriented way of redefining the future with respect to experiencing products and services in context. Hereby, a human-centered perspective is being adopted, where humans are expected not only to be part of systems but also to shape them [HOL 14];

ii) PE strengthens the systemic strategy approach by accentuating the importance of human needs, capabilities and limitations in innovation processes;

iii) PE centers on long-term collaborative advantage. As outcomes are plural and people interact in context, PE intervention promotes collaboration among stakeholders through emergent networks;

iv) PE complements the positivistic characteristics of strategic design by adopting hermeneutic, reflective and participative modes of reasoning to aim for performance and well-being;

v) the generally "post-positivistic" nature of design is given an added dimension through PE intervention, encouraging strategic design to adopt broader views toward innovation but at the same time developing stands;

vi) value creation at individual, organizational, business eco-system and societal levels is being achieved by collaborating well in emergent knowledge networks.

3) As a result, PE offers a more enriched vision on human factors compared to other types of ergonomic interventions. It emphasizes that:

i) new technologies contribute more and more to the development of intangible experiences, which are embodied in services. To develop these innovative experiences, the study and practice of design needs to transition from being object to experience oriented;

ii) ergonomics, which historically has a connection with technology/engineering as well as the social sciences, promotes a broader approach toward innovation than strategic design;

iii) this enriched vision is similar to how different authors perceive PE:

– according to Zink [ZIN 13], ergonomics has been dealing with economic, social and environmental issues but not in a simultaneous and balanced manner;

– several authors claim that a good organizational structure is a prerequisite for systems ergonomics and human factor principles to be effective [GRO 13, SO 13];

– Norros [NOR 14] argues for a systems approach in ergonomics, as well as the need to understand the technology in use in order to promote creativity and learning;

– from a human-computer interaction perspective, Bannon [BAN 11] claims that ergonomics should not only limit itself to the "human technology" fit but consider more the indirect elements that shape people's everyday lives such goals and activities, values, cultures as well as tools and environments;

– the Human Factors and Ergonomics Committee (HFC) under the guidance of Dul *et al.* [DUL 12] redefines the ergonomic profession by applying theoretical principles, data and methods to design in order to optimize human well-being and overall system performance;

– similarly, Robert and Brangier [ROB 09] state that PE focuses on the development of future products and services by anticipating user needs. However, their approach is primarily positivistic, in the sense that the creation of knowledge to explain and predict future events is based upon verified facts. Credibility is solely gained through forward-looking representations of future scenarios or simulated experiments. Somehow, PE has not considered the emergent development of processes, strategies and concepts, as well as their outcomes, which have been initiated through unplanned interactions among stakeholders. This means that the methods and tools which have been put forward and used in PE are mainly positivistic in nature (personas, scenarios, drawings, projection). However, the use of constructivist approaches and methods, such as focus groups, dialogues, creative problem solving workshops, etc., have just been introduced as part of the PE methods and tools package. Therefore, at this point in time it is safe to say that PE is pragmatic in the sense that it aims to necessarily and inevitably construct representations of the future;

– Nelson *et al.* [NEL 12] proposed to align the product development process with different ergonomic interventions. Developed around speculative scenario building and use, PE is being compared with the early stages of the design process, where future products and/or service proposals are sought after;

– Norman [NOR 10] calls for the human systems integration community to mobilize themselves to become proactive designers and solution-givers.

iv) The juxtapositioning of PE and strategic design upon a strategic management platform is very relevant for today's management, ergonomic and design science because interdisciplinary research in the social sciences is being encouraged through globalization trends.

4) A forward looking and future-oriented view in ergonomics may not always be a commonly accepted phenomenon in the field [BAR 62]. However, social demands and current economic issues require improved professional practices, which also count for ergonomics. The various cases, which are presented in this book, highlight some of the newly required practices:

i) ergonomic practitioners need to be more sensitive to social, environmental and political factors when developing human-machine systems;

ii) ergonomic practitioners need to be more proactive in creating and synthesizing innovative products and services;

iii) design practitioners need to understand and consider different management and design perspectives with respect to worldviews before choosing a suitable design approach in their project;

iv) the emphasis on intangibility requires designers to collaborate more actively with ergonomists, sociologists and psychologists to achieve breakthrough innovation;

v) through the connection with design, the ergonomic and management professions are being infused (challenged) with new ways of (creative) thinking and communication;

vi) in terms of education, PE should be taught within the context of design thinking because design thinking refers to design-specific cognitive activities which apply in the design of products, systems, services, organizations and societies. However, PE intervention contributes with a broader foundation for design thinking with respect to worldviews, strategy perspectives, design reasoning mode, processes and methods. Furthermore, the intervention of PE on design thinking also promotes a new way of knowledge transfer, which transitions teaching to mentorship and research to scholarship. For the implementation of a PE-oriented design thinking course, the focus should be more than strategic design and innovation. It should focus on social innovation and value creation by emphasizing and discussing behavioral, cultural, social, technological, ecological and political developments in addition to market and economical situations.

5) Even though there are not many evident cases (4 out of the 12 ergonomic interventions) exemplifying the impact of PE intervention, research in the field should continue to develop along the following perimeters that we are seeking to define:

i) strategic aiming for pluralistic outcomes;

ii) systems driven within a systemic perspective;

iii) human-centered and social innovation oriented.

7.8. Author's perspectives on PE and strategic design

The purpose of this work was to revisit the topics "prospective ergonomics (PE)" and "strategic design" from an overarching strategic/innovation management perspective. Based upon 12 cases, theoretical perspectives on PE have been extended by elucidating the relationship among worldviews, generic strategies and models of design reasoning.

The main idea is that generic innovation strategies as well as strategic design principles extend the field of PE. Pure positivism does not represent a PE approach in developing new products and services. Instead, a combination of positivist and constructivist worldviews is fundamental for adopting PE in a systemic strategy context. Both systemic strategizing and PE acknowledges that innovating is a complex activity bounded by social, technological, economic, environment and political constraints, which may lead to plural outcomes.

Methodologically, PE should adopt a broader perspective toward the development of products and services. With the emergence of constructive ergonomics [FAL 15] and systems ergonomics [WIL 14, DUL 12, EDW 14], the scope of PE can be extended by intervening in the fuzzy front end of innovation. In this way, new alignments are being redefined between PE and strategic design, between preventive ergonomics and industrial design and between corrective ergonomics and detail design (Figure 7.2). The "forward-looking" approach in anticipating innovative products and service, which has been marked as a core element of PE by Robert and Brangier [ROB 09], emerges very well in these new alignments.

However, differences between PE and strategic design have become subtler. Both fields recognize and apply structured processes and prescribed methods as a means to its ends but PE considers the human-centered aspect in its orientation toward innovation. Unlike strategic design, which predominantly aims for profit maximization and problem solving, PE plans for pluralistic outcomes in its innovation process.

To summarize the educational section of this chapter, a PE approach may prepare design students to be better equipped to meet future changes and challenges through the cultivation of their abilities in design management, problem solving, lifelong learning and reflective thinking [SCH 95, FRI 00]. This means that besides scholarly research, the process of being "design active" should be considered as a form of new knowledge creation [FRA 93].

Within knowledge and practice frameworks of PE and strategic design, social, interdisciplinary and inquiry-based learning platforms should be implemented through comprehensive and collaborative studio projects to answer the need for new design themes and to comply with current design processes and methods.   Pedagogically, this may also imply the need for "Vertical Studio Teaching" centered on project-based learning within a master/apprentice relationship [LIE 10], which extends beyond traditional learning by being more inclusive toward the engagement of various stakeholders within specific system contexts.

As a final note in this chapter, I would like to bring up the "prospective turn" in ergonomics, where I consider PE not as "science" but as "design". Instead of planning innovation to be globally and generally focused, PE knowledge should be localized, particular and timely.

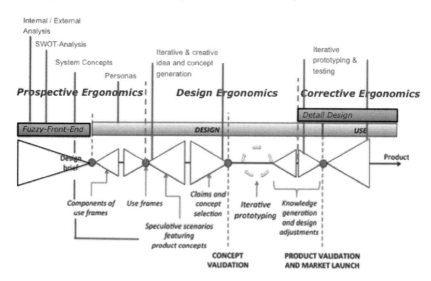

Figure 7.2. *Alignment of the product development process with different ergonomic interventions (adapted from [NEL 13])*

Conclusion and Further Research

Introduction

The need for continued research into PE is considerable, especially considering the paucity of substantial academic work on the subject. In this concluding chapter, the contribution of this research is presented by elucidating how the five research questions have been answered. Furthermore, reflections on limitations and suggestions for future research are given.

Reflections on the research questions

Research question 1

What are the similarities and differences in terms of attitudes and approaches between PE and strategic design, preventive ergonomics and industrial design, corrective ergonomics and detail design?

When comparing PE to strategic design, it can be said that the development of innovative products and services is a common goal in both fields. However, the differences between the two fields are as follows:

– in strategic design, innovation is mostly aimed at profit making, whereas in PE a balance between performance/productivity, on the one hand, and human well-being, on the other hand, is sought after;

– PE aims at developing products which address a product and service which does not exist yet and at anticipating future needs in certain contexts. The aims in strategic design are more diverse, ranging from product extensions to incremental and radical innovation.

In industrial design and preventive ergonomic projects, the main objective is to conceptualize a feasible product or service design based upon a given context and initial design brief. Industrial design approaches the design problem through various perspectives: form, ergonomics, technology, marketing and ecology. However, in preventive ergonomics, user and usability aspects will be emphasized in the design. Common ground between detail design with corrective ergonomics can be found on the level of materialization, where both approaches aim for a realized product. Differences between both fields are similar to the differences between industrial design and preventive ergonomics with respect to design activity.

Research question 2

From a pluralistic business strategy perspective, does the balancing of performance/productivity, on the one hand, and well-being, on the other hand, support the spirit of PE?

In the process of anticipating user needs and imagining future products and services to fulfill these needs, PE seeks the right balance between, on the one hand, profit maximization and, on the other hand, covering the pluralistic objectives of internal and external stakeholders involved in product planning and goal finding.

Furthermore, when adopting a society and business ecosystem perspective, aiming for pluralistic objectives is much more relevant in today's economy. For example, within the context of "network building" and "open innovation", sharing resources may enhance the innovation potential of the entire network as well as their individual actors. Compared to an egocentric and controlled model of strategizing for innovation, a systemic strategy is most relevant for planning innovation activities in business situations, where knowledge and creativity are deliberately facilitated given specific contexts.

Considering a wide range of pluralistic outcomes such as well-being, personal interest and ambitions, family relations, etc., this systemic strategic viewpoint typically characterizes the domain of PE.

Research question 3

Does a systemic business strategy, supported by a structured user-centered and context-driven design approach, represent the field of PE in the development of innovative products, systems and services?

The answer to this research question is partly embedded in the answer of research question 2. However, when the economic objectives of stand-alone organizations are being targeted, prospective ergonomic intervention may also extend toward supporting a classical approach in product planning. However, the intervention of PE within a classical strategy perspective requires organizations to interactively couple push and pull market strategies throughout all stages of the development process. Furthermore, in the coupling of push-pull innovation strategies parallel innovation processes need to be pursued using information technology structures to induce integrated and concurrent product development.

To illustrate the above requirement from a cultural perspective, efficient and targeted interactive parallel innovation processes are difficult for Western companies to emulate where different stakeholders are rationally bounded. This means that individual interests prevail beyond shared ones, which automatically transitions interactive-parallel coupled innovation processes from a classical to a systemic or even less efficient and planned processual strategy mode.

In contrast, Japanese companies, for example, are culturally more adaptable and successful in focusing on more structured innovation activities, where teamwork is being promoted to meet common organizational objectives and deliverables. The above comparative illustration justifies a PE intervention in an uncertain process of new product and service development. Hereby, human-centered and participatory orientations are needed to involve different internal and external stakeholders in a systemic innovation process in which pluralistic objectives are to be met.

Research question 4

To what extent are prescriptive approaches, methods and tools applicable for solving strategic design problems within the context of PE?

Prescriptive approaches, methods and tools in the positivist mode are essential to systematically manage a prospective ergonomic design process. However, these prescriptive approaches should be complemented with constructive modes of reasoning and designing as well as complementary reflective methods and tools. Moreover, the term "problem solving" in the positivistic mode should be contested. Problem solving is a typical design approach, which is supported by a strict design and development process, which may not always align with a more exploratory and anticipative way of designing as intervened by PE.

Research question 5

What are the possible design education strategies, processes, methods and tools to be considered for PE?

Design education strategies, which mainly focus upon the teaching of theoretical concepts, are not sufficient to equip students with the skills required to appropriately respond to the challenges faced by the design industry [HOO 13]. Instead, design educators purposefully train their students to be adaptable by being able to apply a repertoire of theories, techniques and skills in response to their reflective assessment of a typical design context; a competency that Donald Schön refers to as a designer's "artistry" [SCH 87, p. 13].

However, students and novice designers may not always easily comprehend the shift from a theoretical to a practice-based approach in design. They often lack the experience of design practice required to develop contextual and holistic understandings of what they have been taught.

To bridge this gap between design theory and practice, it is necessary to redefine higher "design" education by supporting transitions from teaching to mentorship, research to scholarship and administration to service. The results of these transitions are newly redefined pillars of higher education, which are more transient, integrative and future oriented. These new pillars are most accommodating for design, allowing PE to play a more extensive role in anticipating and creating future needs in systemic contexts. This implies that collaboration with industry and other stakeholders should be emphasized to groom students to manage complex strategic design problems, involving a broader network of stakeholders and targeting different levels of value innovation.

To support such industry collaboration, a team of faculty members and design practitioners should be established who are dedicated to scholarly and practically developing typical prospective ergonomic modes of reasoning, methods and tools to imagine and generate new products and services.

Future research

There are ample opportunities for continuing interdisciplinary research in the field of PE and strategic design. The in-depth exploration of selected management and design frameworks and models as well as analysis of design and design research projects have provided a good starting point for aligning PE with strategic design and repositioning this emergent field of ergonomics within broader contexts of innovation and strategic management. Moreover, this research has attempted to position selected cases within strategic management, worldview, strategic design and design reasoning frameworks.

A very important finding is that prospective ergonomic characteristics apply foremost to projects which are positioned in the systemic strategy quadrant, underlining the collaborative and pragmatic nature of these projects. In these projects, designers complement problem solving approaches with hermeneutic and reflective modes of thinking. With respect to stakeholder involvement and alliance building, these designers advocate the implementation of participatory and creative design methods to anticipate future needs.

However, concerning the development of methods and tools, more empirical data needs to be gathered to ascertain the positioning of PE relative to strategic design within strategic management and innovation frameworks. Examples of research topics which are relevant to be studied to advance the methodology of PE are as follows:

 – the development of systemic frameworks, methods and tools which can be applied across strategic management, strategic design, PE and industrial design;

 – the development of creative methods and tools which can promote lateral thinking in design to anticipate prospective user needs;

 – the creation of design education programs/courses, where an emphasis is placed on bridging the gap between theory and practice in collaborative project work. This means introducing real-life cases and companies as early as possible in the program;

 – the adaptation of prospective ergonomic principles to promote more constructive and reflective ways of designing. Referring to Whittington's processual quadrant as a foundation for one stream of design thinking, what type of emergent strategic and industrial design processes, methods and tools can be developed and what will the prospective ergonomic intervention be?

From a thematic viewpoint, six prospective ergonomic areas, which will be interesting to explore with respect to future research endeavors as well as for the Norwegian economy, will be elaborated in the following sections.

Healthcare and welfare design

Complex healthcare environments render it necessary that a holistic and systematic ergonomic approach be adopted to understand the potential for accidents and errors to occur [BUC 06]. In the last decade, these holistic principles of ergonomics have been employed in different dimensions of the healthcare sector. Ergonomists have advocated to actively consider the needs of all stakeholders by promoting a multifaceted and comprehensive approach in the healthcare sector to minimize the burden of occupational hazards. However, it is unknown whether a prospective-oriented approach toward ergonomic intervention in the healthcare sector has been explored.

Only a few studies have evaluated interventions to reduce injuries among healthcare workers based on worker education programs, physical conditioning, or the use of occupational ergonomic interventions. However, education alone, in the absence of work modifications, is not effective in reducing back injuries among healthcare workers. Physical conditioning, complemented with the utilization of mechanical assistive devices, has therefore been suggested as a preventive ergonomic measure to reduce injuries among healthcare workers [GAR 92, OWE 95, CHA 91, FEL 93].

To promote a holistic value-innovation perspective in the development of the healthcare sector, it is essential to adopt a prospective ergonomic approach to anticipate future products and services. Hereby, it is critical to extend management support to ensure the overall success of the ergonomic process [UNI 15]. In addition, interventions in the form of involvement of workers, patients and other stakeholders through participatory ergonomic and design sessions facilitate early identification of core health issues as well as ancillary arrangements which need to be put in place. A prospective ergonomic intervention in the design of tasks, routines, workspaces, tools, lighting and equipment is needed to match the health workers' physical capabilities and limitations with future patient needs as well as expectations from a broader community of actors who have a stake in healthcare.

In terms of future research in healthcare and welfare design, it would be productive to explore the intersection between "products & services", and "processes and methods" and how a prospective design thinking approach in these two areas may change attitudes, behaviors and norms within occupational ergonomics among the different stakeholders. In practice, this means that in contrast to the more common "top-down" safety programs, participatory ergonomics and design may more effectively take advantage of worker knowledge and problem solving skills, reduce resistance to change and improve workplace communication and worker motivation, as well as facilitate in the anticipation for future products and services [GJE 94, MOO 96].

Inclusive design

According to Clarkson and Coleman [CLA 15, p. 235], inclusive design is designing for disabled and elderly people as a subset of the population and is an integral part of a more recent international trend toward integrating older and disabled people in the mainstream of society.

From a business perspective, design activities should aim at offering high-quality and attractive products and services which may reveal prospective business avenues for imaginative entrepreneurs.

With respect to targeting the public sector and focusing on legislation, it is a challenge to integrate older people as active, participating and contributing members of society in a comparable way to disabled people. This requires us to adopt a consumer-based approach within inclusive design, which is all about developing products and services that delight the end-user rather than stigmatize and alienate them.

Complementing future research plans as described in the section "Reflections on the research questions (see Research questions 1 and 5), it would be interesting to find out what differentiates "good design" from "special needs" design, as well as to generate insights into integrating "good" and "special needs" design.

Good design is about making conscious and well-informed decisions throughout the design process. A great product or service is typically built on a foundation of understanding the real needs of the user and other stakeholders. Within the context of the "business of inclusive design", good design should not aim for pure profit maximization but also target a broader range of objectives within contextual frames of society and legislation.

Service design

The focus in service design is to innovate and improve services which are on the one hand useful, usable and desirable from a user perspective and on the other hand efficient and effective from a management and organizational viewpoint [MAG 11, MOR 05]. More specifically, good service design adds value to user experiences when applied to service sectors such as retailing, banking, transportation and healthcare [STI 10], as well as strategically facilitating a better positioning of service offerings among service providers [MAG 11].

From a strategic management and innovation perspective, service design is less about competition and context and more about reducing the gap between what organizations do and what users expect or need [PAR 06]. Given this aim, services need to be understood as a journey of critical encounters that take place over time and across channels. Hereby, human-to-human or human-to-product interactions centered on "experiencing" before, during and after the service encounter are considered essential.

The human-centered approach investigates or seeks to understand people's experiences as users, service staff and communities or with interactions and practices as a main source for redesigning or imagining new services [MER 11, p. 203].

Users are diverse and possess a wide variety of capabilities, needs and desires. Employees and decision makers within organizations are not simply detached calculating individuals interacting in purely economic transactions but people who are embedded in social relations that may involve their families, state, professional and educational backgrounds, religion and ethnicity [SWE 87, WHI 92].

Within this area, I am planning to make a human-centered strategic link between service design and PE. New theories, frameworks, processes and methods, which should embody this human-centered strategic link, need to be developed and applied in a wide variety of contexts.

Interaction design within the context of culture, acculturation and globalization

"The world is neither a closed system in an ultra-stable steady-state, nor an open one with an inexhaustible supply of energy, water and raw materials, but one whose dynamics calls for a continuing evolution of society, and with it a corresponding evolution of ergonomics and human factor methods to deal with the new problems which will continue to emerge both in the workplace and in society at large" [MOR 00, p. 858].

The above citation clearly presents the ergonomic and cultural challenge with respect to interaction design and social innovation. However, when discussing culture and acculturation in relation to present and future societal developments, the effects of globalization are becoming increasingly evident in the development of services and products. On the one hand, through the influence of multinationals and mass media communication and information, globalization has reached a level of homogeneity among cultures. In other words, globalization strives for cultural compatibility by destroying diversity or ignoring cultural identity. However, some authors like Fernandes [FER 95], appear to be promoting culturalization as a means of opposing "cultural homogenization" by claiming that the global process of homogenization may provoke people to be more aware of their national and cultural identities.

On the other hand, globalization can be seen as a motivator for some originally homogenous societies to become heterogeneous multicultural societies. Some societies have embraced globalization, while others oppose it or are selective [SHE 06].

The above discussion poses the question of whether a localization or globalization approach should be adopted in the development of products, services and human-computer interaction interfaces with respect to enhancement of the user experience.

For future research, I am proposing to further develop a methodology for strategic goal finding based upon acculturation insights, derived from social, cultural, technological, economic and political differences among regions. The development of such a methodology implies the selection of empirical research methods to gain better insights on how to design products, user interfaces and services, bearing in mind cultural differences and globalization trends. These methods are as follows:

– persona development and selection;

– scenario building and reflection;

– cultural confrontation of scenarios;

– case study research.

In my past case study research work, the diversity of case studies, each leading to a proposed design concept, has demonstrated that a cultural and contextual approach toward strategic design should be further explored in the development of user interface systems and products in the Fuzzy-Front-End of Innovation (FEI).

The process of illustrating framed cases and assessing possible extreme social, political and economical effects in certain societies can identify potential areas for innovation. The framing and assessment occur by mapping showing extreme situations of a case on a bipolar scale, supported by cultural dimensions.

The purpose of developing these methods in a more integrative manner is to build a database of cases, to be refined and updated from time-to-time, which can be further developed into a methodology for creative inspiration in the product planning and goal finding stages of the strategic design process. In other words, once matured, such a database comprising diverse cases can be used as a resource for deepening the external analysis as well as generating innovative system/product ideas, while considering the prevalent economic, social and political status quo of cultures. Furthermore, theme-specific cases can be clustered to develop cultural bipolar scales as a source to better understand global tension fields with respect to social, economic, political and environmental developments worldwide.

Aesthetics and experience design

User experience influences the individual's belief about himself/herself and his/her physical appearance. It is conceived as the sensation of how someone perceives and interprets something that they are surrounded by and how one sees possibilities for the next interaction [PHO 15].

User experience encompasses more than just satisfaction. Satisfaction is associated directly with aesthetics, which has to do with emotions, a common quality between aesthetics and user satisfaction [NIE 99].

The individual's judgment about aesthetics, beauty, or what is pleasing is based upon personal, social and cultural background (user experience).

However, recent research has shown that the positive effect of an aesthetically appealing product on perceived usability begins to wane with increasing exposure time [SON 12]. This means that focusing on corrective and preventive ergonomics has its limitations in the design of aesthetic-driven products with respect to prospection.

Aesthetics and meaning-making research should therefore be conducted within the context of innovation. In other words, my research interest within this area is driven by the notion that consumers in mature economies are always enticed by the emotional qualities of a product. To be more specific, they are scouting for forms which embody new meanings and aesthetics. Within the context of "pleasurable" experiences, which forms the foundation for research in meaning-making and aesthetics, personal, cultural and emotional aspects as well as systemic constraints and possibilities should be addressed in the development of new products and services.

Transportation design

Transportation in its many forms has undergone significant transformations to meet the needs of a changing age-diverse society, which has implications for design, research and policies for both older and younger adults across a broad range of contexts.

For example, baby boomers prefer personal transportation specifically in the form of a personal vehicle because of the following two reasons:

– they find it hard and confusing to use crowdsourcing and app-based transportation guidance, making public transportation navigation and use a frustrating experience;

– most likely, they prefer to use private transportation because they live in areas that do not have good public transportation [DEG 11, FIS 09, TUR 12].

On the contrary, the younger population is driving less and frequently uses public transportation, ride sharing and other transportation alternatives. They consistently respond well to crowdsourcing and app-based transportation guidance [DAV 12, DEL 13, PUE 12]. These needs require researchers to evaluate the design of systems to manage the conflicting desires, abilities, cultural and demographic factors, as well as personal goals related to different age groups from anywhere between 20 to 60 years. In these systemic cases, it might be productive to create either adaptable or redundant systems where way-finding guidance is included in the physical environment of transportation hubs.

As the health and activity gap between older and younger adults is narrowing, it has become easier to introduce inclusive design solutions. However, this may not be the case for all in-vehicle automation situations where human factor solutions for one typical age group may not apply for another. For instance, augmented in-vehicle automation, which is accepted and desired by tech-savvy youth, may lead to overreliance and subsequently skill degradation [PAR 97]. On the contrary, older adults are more averse to automation and resistant to advances such as automatic braking and self-driving cars. At the same time, age deteriorates the sensory abilities to perceive safety-critical alarms. For example, an alarm that is loud enough to be reliably heard by a driver in her 70s may be extremely intrusive to a much younger driver.

Another example showing different views with respect to vehicle design concerns the design and development of special vehicles such as fire engines, police cars and ambulances. Two different approaches can be identified in the interior design and customization of these vehicles. The first is defined as vehicle integrative customization and the second as vehicle adaptive customization. Integrative customization in vehicle design is the implementation of various equipment and devices without compromising on the existing features and space. It is only practically achievable when the design, fabrication and installation of the customized features have been completed in concurrence with the manufacturing of the vehicle itself. On the other hand, adaptive customization in vehicle design can be implemented during or at any stage after the manufacturing of the vehicle. This implies that the quality of adaptive customization may vary from a crude add-on to a neatly hidden solution, such as the placement of equipment behind the cladding/dashboard of the vehicle.

The above examples show that there are clear tension fields in the areas of transportation and vehicle design which are befitted to be solved through innovative product service systems solutions, where prospective ergonomic intervention is considered to be essential.

Summary of future research directions, relevant for prospective ergonomics

Figure 1 shows a consolidated view of my intended future research work centered on PE. I am particularly interested in how prospective ergonomic intervention should contribute to each of the six thematic fields through research and design. With respect to each field, I am targeting the juxtaposition of (1) processes, methods and tools, (2) perspectives and mindsets and (3) challenges as focal areas for reflection with PE (see Figure 1).

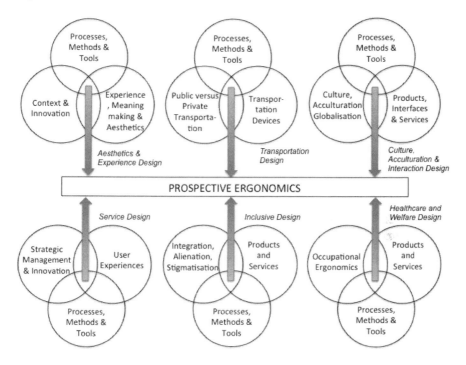

Figure 1. *Relations between specific "processes, methods and tools", "perspectives and mindsets" and "challenges", and how an integrated view connects with prospective ergonomics*

Case example: versatile mailbox

From a practice point of view, I would like to introduce a design project which illustrates the connectivity between service, welfare and transportation design within the context of prospective ergonomics. The project concerns the development of a "versatile mailbox" (Postkasse 3.0) which extends the delivery of non-perishable objects to include medication and perishable items (Figure 2). Besides the functional aspects of mail delivery, the overarching social, technological, economic, environmental and political context of a social-democratic society, such as Norway, will be challenged.

From current to future context

Increasing levels of e-commerce, transitioning from paper mail to digital mail, rising popularity for food delivery and new markets allowing for delivery of medication fundamentally restructure public life and require a rethinking of the functionality of mailboxes (Figure 2).

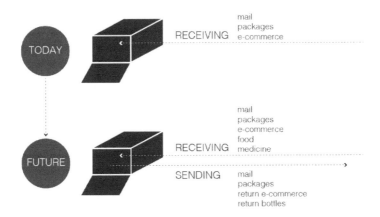

Figure 2. *Transitioning from the current to a future versatile mailbox*

– What if mailboxes could receive and send items?

– What if the inside of mailboxes could be controlled to ensure a specified temperature range?

– What if everything could arrive right at the door step whether someone is home or not?

Project brief

The "versatile mailbox" (Postkasse 3.0) is intended to explore such possibilities and aims to redefine the mailbox as a place of mutual exchange.

When rethinking the mailbox in a future Norwegian context, it becomes obvious that it would make a mailbox more relevant if its functionality would include sending besides only receiving goods. Such a development would make the mailbox a more meaningful place of exchange, facilitating e-commerce through, for example, simplifying receiving and returning of desired items. As such, postal activities will be decentralized and relocated to the home of the individual, rendering him or her able to send and receive packages without making trips to the nearest post office.

Creating such a medium of exchange, allowing for secure and controlled storage, opens new business opportunities for food and medication delivery as well as the provision of specialized nutrition to elderly people with specific dietary needs.

PRIVATE REALM

Elderly
Sick people
Disabled people
Busy professionals
Families
Students

POSTKASSE 3.0

PUBLIC REALM

Posten
Post Nord
Pharmacies
Grocery Delivery
Health care services

Figure 3. *The mailbox is positioned at the intersection of the private and the public realm*

As per today, the mailbox is positioned at the intersection of the private and the public realm (Figure 3). It would facilitate the participation of a wider range of stakeholders by creating meaningful and relevant services for its owners and increased operational efficiency for different service providers.

Processes, methods and stakeholder involvement

The project scope was limited to an extensive design research and concept generation process. In the design research stage, semistructured interviews were undertaken with different stakeholders. These stakeholders include public and private postal services, pharmacists, city councils, care takers, elderly homes, grocery home delivery services, etc. In the idea generation and conceptualization stages, different scenarios and design proposals were sketched and subjected to potential stakeholders in individual one-to-one as well as group participatory sessions.

Figure 4 exemplifies a schematic diagram of the relationships among the various stakeholders, where the "versatile mailbox" functions as facilitation platform for the exchange of goods and services. The diagram illustrates the variety of private and public actors benefitting from the service potential it provides. While the left side of the illustration focuses on businesses and organizations, the right side highlights various end user groups. After having identified these stakeholder groups, the graph can visually represent how individual actors can be coupled in order to offer service innovations, such as food delivery or advanced home medication for elderly.

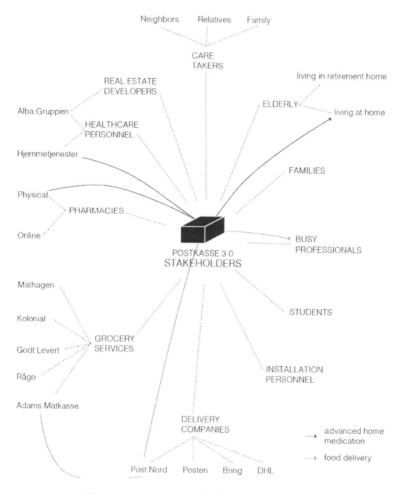

Figure 4. *Future stakeholder constellation centered around the "versatile mailbox"*

Results

Rethinking parcel delivery, however, does not necessarily mean having mailboxes as physical interfaces between the public and the private realm. For example, the Antwerp-based company "Cardrops" uses the car of the parcel recipient as interface.

Most importantly, the versatile mailbox should be perceived as a pivotal point between the private and public realm within a larger product service system improving the convenience of home delivery. The Norwegian private and public service sector is currently being subjected to significant challenges. A tremendous growth in the food delivery sector as well as new regulations in the medication market and rising popularity of e-commerce requires innovative distribution channels. The "versatile mailbox" is one of them, aimed at dual income families coupled with busy schedules and the elderly with limited mobility. Moreover, on the service provision side, it aims to alleviate the pressure on delivery companies to deliver goods at predetermined and selective timeslots.

Bibliography

[ABE 94] ABERCROMBIE N., HILL S., TURNER B.S., *Dictionary of Sociology*, 3rd edition, Penguin, UK, 1994.

[ABE 74] ABERNATHY W.J., WAYNE K., "Limits of the learning curve", *Harvard Business Review*, vol. 52, no. 5, pp. 109–119, 1974.

[AGO 14] AGOGUE M., KAZAKCI A., "10 years of C-K theory: a survey on the academic and industrial impacts of a design theory", in CHAKRABARTI A., BLESSING L. (eds), *An Anthology of Theories and Models of Design*, Springer, London, 2014.

[ALT 09] ALTBACH P.G., REISBERG L., RUMBLEY L.E., "Trends in global higher education, Tracking an academic revolution", *UNESCO 2009 World Conference on Higher Education*, SIDA/SAREC, 2009.

[AMA 96] AMABILE T.M., CONTI R., COON H. *et al.*, "Assessing the work environment for creativity", *Academy of Management Journal*, vol. 39, no. 5, pp. 1154–1184, 1996.

[AND 71] ANDREWS K.R., *The Concept of Corporate Strategy*, revised edition, Richard D. Irwin, US, 1971.

[ANS 68] ANSOFF H.I., *Corporate Strategy: An Analytic Approach to Business Policy for Growth and Expansion*, Penguin, 1968.

[ANS 80] ANSOFF H.I., "Strategic issue management", *Strategic Management Journal*, vol. 1, no. 2, pp. 131–148, 1980.

[BAL 89] BALAKIER J.J., "Thomas Traherne's dobell series and the Baconian model of experience", *English Studies*, vol. 70, no. 3, pp. 233–247, 1989.

[BAL 99] BALDWIN J.L., "Mentoring", *Bulletin of the King County Medical Society*, pp. 5–6, 1999.

[BAM 02] BAMFORD G., "From analysis/synthesis to conjecture/analysis: a review of Karl Popper's influence on design methodology in architecture", *Design Studies*, vol. 23, no. 3, pp. 245–261, 2002.

[BAN 02] BANNON L., "Taking "Human-Centered Computing" Seriously", *COCONET: Context-Aware Collaborative Environments for Next Generation Business Networks*, Helsinki, 2002.

[BAN 11] BANNON L., "Reimagining HCI: toward a more human-centred perspective", *Interactions*, vol. 18, no. 4, pp. 50–57, 2011.

[BAN 15] BANNON L., CARVALHO P., GOMES J.O. *et al.*, "Expanding ergonomics: prospects and pitfalls", *Proceedings of the 19th Triennial Congress of the IEA*, vol. 9, p. 14, 2015.

[BAR 91] BARNEY J., "Firm resources and sustained competitive advantage", *Journal of Management*, vol. 17, no. 1, pp. 99–120, 1991.

[BAR 62] BARTLETT F.C., "Ergonomics research society: the society's lecture", *Ergonomics*, vol. 5, no. 4, pp. 505–511, 1962.

[BEL 04] BELLIVEAU P., GRIFFIN A., SOMERMEYER S., *The PDMA Toolbook 1 for New Product Development*, John Wiley & Sons, New York, 2004.

[BHA 00] BHAGIA J., TINSLEY J.A., "The mentoring partnership", *Mayo Clinic Proceedings*, vol. 75, no. 5, pp. 535–537, 2000.

[BLO 05] BLOOM D.E., "Raising the pressure: globalization and the need for higher education reform", in JONES A., MCCARNEY P., SKOLNIK M. (eds), *Creating Knowledge, Strengthening Nations: The Changing Role of Higher Education*, University of Toronto Press, 2005.

[BON 09] BONNARDEL N., "Activités de conception et créativité : de l'analyse des facteurs cognitifs à l'assistance aux activités de conception créatives", *Le Travail Humain*, vol. 72, no. 1, pp. 5–22, 2009.

[BOY 90] BOYER E., *Scholarship Reconsidered: Priorities of the Professorate*, The Carnegie Foundation for the Advancement of Teaching, New Jersey, 1990.

[BRA 04] BRANDT E., MESSETER J., "Facilitating collaboration through design games", *Proceedings of the Eighth Conference on Participatory Design: Artful Integration: Interweaving Media, Materials and Practices*, vol. 1, pp. 121–131, ACM, Canada, 2004.

[BRA 10] BRANGIER E., ROBERT J.M., "Confèrence pour l'ergonomie prospective: Anticiper de futures activités humaines en vue de concevoir de nouveaux artéfacts" *Conference Internationale Francophone sur l'Interaction Homme-Machine*, pp. 57–64, ACM, Luxemburg, 2010.

[BRA 12] BRANGIER E., ROBERT J.M., "L'innovation par l'ergonomie: éléments d'ergonomie prospective", in LLERENA D., RIEN D. (eds), *Innovation, Connaissances et Société: Vers une Société de L'innovation*, L'Harmattan, Paris, 2012.

[BRA 14] BRANGIER E., ROBERT J.M., "L'ergonomie prospective: fondements et enjeux", *Le Travail Humain*, vol. 77, no. 1, pp. 1–20, 2014.

[BRO 97] BROBERG O., "Integrating ergonomics into the product development process", *International Journal of Industrial Ergonomics*, vol. 19, no. 4, pp. 317–327, 1997.

[BRO 89] BROWN J.S., COLLINS A., DUGUID P., "Situated Cognition and the Culture of Learning", *Education Researcher*, vol. 18, no. 1, pp. 32–42, 1989.

[BRO 91] BROWN J.S., DUGUID P., "Organizational learning and communities-of-practice: Toward a unified view of working, learning, and innovation", *Organization Science*, vol. 2, no. 1, pp. 40–57, 1991.

[BRU 00] BRUDER R., "Ergonomics as mediator within the product design process", *Human Factors and Ergonomics Society Annual Meeting*, vol. 44, no. 8, pp. 20–23, 2000.

[BUC 11] BUCKLE P., BUCKLE J., "Obesity, ergonomics and public health", *Perspectives in Public Health*, vol. 131, no. 4, pp. 170–176, 2011.

[BUC 06] BUCKLE P., CLARKSON P.J., COLEMAN R. *et al.*, "Patient safety, systems design and ergonomics", *Applied Ergonomics*, vol. 37, no. 4, pp. 491–500, 2006.

[BUI 87] BUIJS J.A., *Innovatie en Interventie*, 2nd edition, Kluwer, Deventer, 1987.

[BUI 96] BUIJS J.A., VALKENBURG A.C., *Integrale Produktontwikkeling*, Utrecht Lemma, The Netherlands, 1996.

[BUR 10] BURR V., *Social Construction*, 2nd edition, Routledge, New York, 2010.

[CAG 02] CAGAN J., VOGEL C.M., *Creating Breakthrough Products: Innovation from Product Planning to Program Approval*, Prentice Hall, New Jersey, 2002.

[CAP 08] CAPLE D., "Emerging challenges to the ergonomics domain", *Ergonomics*, vol. 51, no. 1, pp. 49–54, 2008.

[CAR 06] CARAYON P., "Human factors of complex sociotechnical systems", *Applied Ergonomics*, vol. 37, no. 4, pp. 525–535, 2006.

[CHA 93] CHAFFIN D.B., ANDERSON G.B.J., *Occupational Biomechanics*, 2nd edition, Wiley-Interscience, New Jersey, 1993.

[CHA 05] CHAN KIM W., MAUBORGNE R., "Value innovation: a leap into the blue ocean", *Journal of Business Strategy*, vol. 26, no. 4, pp. 22–28, 2005.

[CHA 91] CHARNEY W., ZIMMERMAN K., WALARA E., "The lifting team. A design method to reduce lost time back injury in nursing", *AAOHN Journal: Official Journal of the American Association of Occupational Health Nurses*, vol. 39, no. 5, pp. 231–234, 1991.

[CHE 02] CHESBROUGH H., ROSENBLOOM R.S., "The role of the business model in capturing value from innovation: evidence from Xerox Corporation's technology spin-off companies", *Industrial and Corporate Change*, vol. 11, no. 3, pp. 529–555, 2002.

[CHR 13] CHRISTENSEN C., *The Innovator's Dilemma: When New Technologies Cause Great Firms to Fail*, Harvard Business Review Press, Boston, 2013.

[CHR 00] CHRISTIANSEN J.A., *Building the Innovative Organization*, MacMillan Press, London, 2000.

[CLA 15] CLARKSON P.J., COLEMAN R., "History of Inclusive Design in the UK", *Applied Ergonomics*, vol. 46, part B, pp. 235–247, 2015.

[CLA 11] CLAUSEN T., POHJOLA M., SAPPRASERT K. *et al.*, "Innovation strategies as a source of persistent innovation", *Industrial and Corporate Change*, vol. 21, no. 3, pp. 553–585, 2011.

[COU 00] I.E.A. COUNCIL, "The discipline of ergonomics", *International Ergonomics Society*, vol. 1, pp. 3–37, 2000.

[CRE 09] CRESWELL J.W., *Research design: Qualitative, Quantitative, and Mixed Methods Approaches*, Sage Publications, Los Angeles, 2009.

[CRO 11] CROWE S., CRESSWELL K., ROBERTSON A. *et al.*, "The case study approach", *BMC Medical Research Methodology*, vol. 11, no. 1, 2011.

[CUP 01] CUPCHIK G., "Constructivist realism: an ontology that encompasses positivist and constructivist approaches to the social sciences", *Forum: Qualitative Social Research*, vol. 2, no. 1, 2001.

[CYE 63] CYERT R., MARCH J., *A Behavioral Theory of the Firm*, Englewood Cliffs, Prentice-Hall, New Jersey, 1963.

[DAM 91] DAMANPOUR F., "Organizational innovation: a meta-analysis of effects of determinants and moderators", *Academy of Management Journal*, vol. 34, no. 3, pp. 555–590, 1991.

[DAR 79] DARKE J., "The primary generator and the design process", *Design Studies*, vol. 1, no. 1, pp. 36–44, 1979.

[DAV 12] DAVIS B., DUTZIK T., BAXANDALL P., Transportation and the new generation: Why young people are driving less and what it means for transportation policy, Report, The National Academies of Sciences, Engineering and Medicine, Washington, DC, 2012.

[DEG 11] DEGOOD K., Aging in place, stuck without options: Fixing the mobility crisis threatening the baby boom generation, Report, The National Academies of Science, Engineering and Medicine, Washington, DC, 2011.

[DEL 13] DELBOSC A., CURRIE G., "Causes of youth licensing decline: a synthesis of evidence", *Transport Reviews*, vol. 33, no. 3, pp. 271–290, 2013.

[DEL 10] DELIOS A., "How can organizations be competitive but dare to care?", *The Academy of Management Perspectives*, vol. 24, no. 3, pp. 25–36, 2010.

[DES 06] DESIGN COUNCIL, Creative & cultural skills, design a new design industry: design skills consultation, UK Design Industry Skills Development Plan, 2006.

[DIA 04] DIAPER D., STANTON N.A., *The Handbook of Task Analysis for Human–Computer Interaction*, Lawrence Erlbaum Associates, New Jersey, 2004.

[DOS 82] DOSI G., "Technological paradigms and technological trajectories: a suggested interpretation of the determinants and directions of technical change", *Research Policy*, vol. 11, no. 3, pp. 147–62, 1982.

[DRA 85] DRAY S., "Macroergonmics in organizations: An introduction", in BROWN I.D., GOLDSMITH R., COMBES K. *et al.* (eds), *Ergonomics International*, pp. 520–522, 1985.

[DRU 54] DRUCKER P.F., *The Practice of Management*, Harper & Row, New York, 1954.

[DRU 08] DRURY C.G., "The future of ergonomics/the future of work: 45 years after Bartlett (1962)", *Ergonomics*, vol. 51, no. 1, pp. 14–20, 2008.

[DUL 11] DUL J., CEYLAN C., "Work environments for employee creativity", *Ergonomics*, vol. 54, no. 1, pp. 12–20, 2011.

[DUL 09] DUL J., NEUMANN W.P., "Ergonomic contributions to company strategies", *Applied Ergonomics*, vol. 40, no. 4, pp. 745–752, 2009.

[DUL 12] DUL J., BRUDER R., BUCKLE P. *et al.*, "A strategy for human factors/ergonomics: developing the discipline and profession", *Ergonomics*, vol. 55, no. 4, pp. 377–395, 2012.

[EDW 01] EDWARD H., BOWMAN H.S., THOMAS H., "The domain of strategic management: history and evolution", *Handbook of Strategy and Management*, vol. 3, pp. 31–51, 2001.

[EDW 14] EDWARDS K., JENSEN P.L., "Design of systems for productivity and well being", *Applied Ergonomics*, vol. 45, no. 1, pp. 26–32, 2014.

[EIN 81] EINHORN H.J., HOGARTH R.M., "Behavioral decision theory: processes of judgment and choice", *Journal of Accounting Research*, vol. 19, no. 1, pp. 1–31, 1981.

[EIS 89] EISENHARDT K.M., "Building theories from case study research", *Academy of Management Review*, vol. 14, no. 4, pp. 532–550, 1989.

[EME 60] EMERY F.E., TRIST E.L., "Socio-technical systems", in CHURCHMAN W., VERHULST M. (eds), *Management Sciences, Models and Techniques*, vol. 2, pp. 83–97, Pergamon Press, London, 1960.

[END 04] ENDERS J., "Higher education, internationalisation, and the nation-state: Recent developments and challenges to governance theory", *Higher Education*, vol. 47, no. 3, pp. 361–382, 2004.

[ESS 11] ESSLINGER H., "Sustainable design: beyond the innovation-driven business model", *Journal of Product Innovation Management*, vol. 28, no. 3, pp. 401–404, 2011.

[ETZ 97] ETZKOWITZ H., LEYTESDORFF L., *Universities in the Global Economy: A Triple Helix of Academic-Industry-Government Relation*, Croom Helm, London, 1997.

[FAL 07] FALZON P., MAS L., "Les objectifs de l'ergonomie et les objectifs des ergonomes", in ZOUINAR M., VALLÉRY G., LE PORT M.-C. (eds), *Ergonomie des Produits et des Services, 42e Congrès de la SELF*, Toulouse, 2007.

[FAL 15] FALZON P., *Constructive Ergonomics*. CRC Press, Boca Raton, 2015.

[FEL 93] FELDSTEIN A., VALANIS B., VOLLMER W. *et al.*, "The back injury prevention project pilot study: assessing the effectiveness of Back Attack, an injury prevention program among nurses, aides, and orderlies", *Journal of Occupational and Environmental Medicine*, vol. 35, no. 2, p. 114, 1993.

[FER 95] FERNANDES T., *Global interface design: A guide to designing international user interfaces*, AP Professional, New York, 1995.

[FIN 09] FINGAR C.T., *Global trends 2025: A Transformed World*, DIANE Publishing, Washington D.C., 2009.

[FIS 09] FISK A.D., ROGERS W.A., CHARNESS N. *et al.*, *Designing for Older Adults: Principles and Creative Human Factors Approaches*, CRC Press, Boca Raton, 2009.

[FLY 06] FLYVBJERG B., "Five misunderstandings about case-study research", *Qualitative Inquiry*, vol. 12, no. 2, pp. 219–245, 2006.

[FOG 09] FOGG B.J., "A behavior model for persuasive design", *Proceedings of the 4th International Conference on Persuasive Technology*, p. 40, ACM, New York, 2009.

[FRA 93] FRAYLING C., *Research in Art and Design*, Royal College of Art, London, 1993.

[FRI 01] FRIEDMAN K., "Design education in the university: professional studies for the knowledge economy", in SWANN C., YOUNG E. (eds), *Re-inventing Design Education in the University*, *Proceedings of the Perth International Conference*, Curtin University of Technology, pp. 14–28, 2001.

[GAR 92] GARG A., OWEN B., "Reducing back stress to nursing personnel: an ergonomic intervention in a nursing home", *Ergonomics*, vol. 35, no. 11, pp. 1353–1375., 1992.

[GEE 04] GEELS F.W., "From sectoral systems of innovation to socio-technical systems. insights about dynamics and change from sociology and institutional theory", *Research Policy*, vol. 33, pp. 897–920, 2004.

[GER 88] GERSICK C.J., "Time and transition in work teams: Toward a new model of group development", *Academy of Management Journal*, vol. 31, no. 1, pp. 9–41, 1988.

[GHE 02] GHEMAWAT P., "Competition and business strategy in historical perspective", *Business History Review*, vol. 76, no. 1, pp. 37–74, 2002.

[GIB 06] GIBSON C.B., GIBBS J.L., "Unpacking the concept of virtuality: The effects of geographic dispersion, electronic dependence, dynamic structure, and national diversity on team innovation", *Administrative Science Quarterly*, vol. 51, no. 3, pp. 451–495, 2006.

[GJE 94] GJESSING C.C., SCHOENBORN T.F., COHEN A., Participatory Ergonomic Interventions in Meatpacking Plants, US Department of Health and Human Services, 1994.

[GLA 67] GLASER B., STRAUSS A., *The Discovery of Grounded Theory: Strategies of Qualitative Research,* Aldine Publishing Company, New York, 1967.

[GOT 96] GODET M., ROUBELAT F., "Creating the future: the use and misuse of scenarios", *Long Range Planning*, vol. 29, no. 2, pp. 164–171, 1996.

[GOR 04] GORDON T., GLENN J., "Integration, Comparisons, and Frontiers of Futures Research Methods", EU-US Seminar: New Technology Foresight, Forecasting and Assessment Methods, Seville, 2004.

[GRA 85] GRANOVETTER M., "Economic action and social structure: the problem of embeddedness", *American Journal of Sociology*, vol. 91, no. 3, pp. 481–510, 1985.

[GRO 14] GROTE G., "Adding a strategic edge to human factors/ergonomics: Principles for the management of uncertainty as cornerstones for system design", *Applied Ergonomics*, vol. 45, no. 1, pp. 33–39, 2014.

[HAR 86] HARRIS S.G., SUTTON R.I., "Functions of parting ceremonies in dying organizations", *Academy of Management Journal*, vol. 29, no. 1, pp. 5–30, 1986.

[HAT 03] HATCHUEL A., WEIL B., "A New Approach of Innovative Design: an Introduction to CK Theory", *DS 31: Proceedings of ICED 03, the 14th International Conference on Engineering Design,* pp. 109–110, Stockholm, 2003.

[HAT 10] HATCHUEL A., STARKEY K., TEMPEST S. *et al.*, "Strategy as innovative design: an emerging perspective", in BAUM JOEL A.C., LAMPEL J. (eds), *The Globalization of Strategy Research, (Advances in Strategic Management,* vol. 27, pp. 3–28, Emerlad Group Publishing, 2010.

[HAY 80] HAYNES R., ABERNATHY W., "Managing our way to economic decline", *Harvard Business Review*, pp. 67–77, July–August 1980.

[HED 08] HEDGE A., SPIER A.L., "On the future of ergonomics: HFES members speak out", *HFES Bulletin*, vol. 51, no. 2, pp. 1–2, 2008.

[HEL 95] HELANDER M.G., *A Guide to Ergonomics and Manufacturing*, Taylor and Francis, London, 1995.

[HEL 97] HELANDER M.G., "The human factors profession", in SALVENDY G. (ed.), *Handbook of Human Factors and Ergonomics*, 2nd edition, John Wiley & Sons, New York, 1997.

[HEN 79] HENDERSON B.D., *On Corporate Strategy*, Abt Books, Massachusetts, 1979.

[HEN 84] HENDERSON B.D., *The Logic of Business Strategy*, Ballinger Publishing Massachusetts, 1984.

[HEN 86] HENDRICK H.W., "Macroergonomics: a conceptual model for integrating human factors with organizational design", in BROWN JR. O., HENDRICK H.W. (eds), *Human Factors in Organizational Design and Management II*, pp. 467–478, Elsevier Science, Amsterdam, 1986.

[HEN 91] HENDRICK H.W., "Ergonomics in organizational design and management", *Ergonomics,* vol. 34, no. 6, pp. 743–756, 1991.

[HEN 01] HENDRICK H.W., KLEINER B.M., *Macroergonomics: An Introduction to Work System Design,* Human Factors and Ergonomics Society, Santa Monica, CA, 2001.

[HIE 11a] HIENERT D., SCHAER P., SCHAIBLE J. *et al.*, "A novel combined term suggestion service for domain-specific digital libraries", in GRADMANN S., BORRI F., MEGHINI C. *et al.* (eds), *Research and Advanced Technology for Digital Libraries,* pp. 192–203, Springer, Berlin-Heidelberg, 2011.

[HIE 11b] HIENERTH C., KEINZ P., LETTL C., "Exploring the nature and implementation process of user-centric business models", *Long Range Planning*, vol. 44, no. 5, pp. 344–374, 2011.

[HOL 99] HOLBROOK M.B., *Consumer Value: A Framework for Analysis and Research*, Psychology Press, Routledge, London, 1999.

[HOL 03] HOLLNAGEL E., *Handbook of Cognitive Task Design*, Lawrence Erlbaum Associates, Mahwah, 2003.

[HOL 05] HOLLNAGEL E., WOODS D.D., *Joint Cognitive Systems: Foundations of Cognitive Systems Engineering*, CRC Press, Boca Raton, 2005.

[HOL 14] HOLLNAGEL E., "Human factors/ergonomics as a systems discipline?, the human use of human beings", *Applied Ergonomics*, vol. 45, no. 1, pp. 40–44, 2014.

[HOL 03] HOLMAN D., WALL T.D., CLEGG C.W. *et al.*, *The New Workplace: A Guide to the Human Impact of Modern Working Practices,* John Wiley & Sons, New Jersey, 2003.

[HOO 13] HOOK J., HJERMITSLEV T., IVERSEN O.S. *et al.*, "The ReflecTable: bridging the gap between theory and practice in design education", in PAULA K., GARY M., GITTE L. *et al.* (eds), *Human-Computer Interaction–INTERACT*, Springer, Berlin-Heidelberg, 2013.

[IMA 86] IMADA A.S., NORO K., NAGAMACHI M., "Participatory ergonomics: methods for improving individual and organizational effectiveness", in BROWN JR. O., HENDRICK H.W. (eds), *Human Factors in Organizational Design and Management II*, Elsevier-Science, Amsterdam, 1986.

[JAP 06] JAPAN ERGONOMICS SOCIETY, The JES Ergonomics Roadmap, Japan Ergonomics Society, Japan, 2006.

[KAP 90] KAPOR M., "A software design manifesto", *Dr. Dobb's Journal*, vol. 16, no. 1, pp. 62–67, 1990.

[KAR 98] KARWOWSKI W., "Selected directions and trends in development of ergonomics in USA", *Ergonomia*, vol. 21, nos. 1–2, pp. 141–155, Krakow, 1998.

[KAR 05] KARWOWSKI W., "Ergonomics and human factors: the paradigms for science, engineering, design, technology and management of human-compatible systems", *Ergonomics*, vol. 48, no. 5, pp. 436–463, 2005.

[KAR 06] KARWOWSKI W., "From past to future: building a collective vision for HFES 2020+", *HFES Bulletin*, vol. 49, no. 11, pp. 1–3, 2006.

[KAR 12] KARWOWSKI W., "The discipline of human factors and ergonomics", in SALVENDY G. (ed.), *Handbook of Human Factors and Ergonomics*, 4th edition, pp. 3–37, John Wiley & Sons, New Jersey, 2012.

[KAR 98] KARWOWSKI W., MARRAS W.S., *The Occupational Ergonomics Handbook*, CRC Press, 1998.

[KID 82] KIDDER T., *Soul of a New Machine*, Avon, New York, 1982.

[KJE 10] KJELDSTADLI K., *Akademisk Kapitalisme*, Res Publica, Norway, 2010.

[KOL 14] KOLB D.A., *Experiential Learning: Experience as the Source of Learning and Development*, FT Press, New Jersey, 2014.

[KON 92] KONZ S., "Macro-ergonomic guidelines for production planning", in HELANDER M., NAGAMACHI M. (eds), *Design for Manufacturability*, Taylor & Francis, London, 1992.

[KRI 06] KRIPPENDORFF K., *The Semantic Turn. A New Foundation for Design*, CRC Taylor & Francis, Boca Raton, 2006.

[KRI 02] KRISTENSSON P., MAGNUSSON P.R., MATTHING J., "Users as a hidden resource for creativity: findings from an experimental study on user involvement", *Creativity and Innovation Management*, vol. 11, no. 1, pp. 55–61, 2002.

[KRO 94] KROEMER K., KROEMER H., KROEMER-ELBERT K., *Ergonomics: How to Design for Ease and Efficiency*, Prentice-Hall, New Jersey, 1994.

[KYF 03] KYFFIN S., NewValueNews, no. 18, Philips Design, October 2003.

[LAN 95] LANDRY M., "A note on the concept of problem", *Organization Studies*, vol. 16, no. 2, pp. 315–343, 1985.

[LAU 86] LAURIG W., "Prospective ergonomics: new approach to industrial ergonomics", in KARWOWSKI W. (ed.), *Trends in Ergonomics: Human Factors III*, Elsevier Science, Amsterdam, 1986.

[LAU 00] LAURILLARD D., "Students and the curriculum", in SCOTT P. (ed.), *Higher Education Re-formed*, Falmer Press, London, 2000.

[LAV 91] LAVE J., WENGER E., *Situated Learning: Legitimate Peripheral Participation*, Cambridge University Press, 1991.

[LEV 60] LEVITT T., "Marketing myopia", *Harvard Business Review*, vol. 38, no. 4, pp. 24–47, 1960.

[LEW 02] LEWIS W.P., BONOLLO E., "An analysis of professional skills in design: implications for education and research", *Design Studies*, vol. 23, no. 4, pp. 385–406, 2002.

[LIE 00] LIEDTKA J., "In defense of strategy as design", *California Management Review*, vol. 42, no. 3, pp. 8–30, 2000.

[LIE 08] LIEM A., "Developing a win-win mentorship-scholarship, higher education model for design through collaborative learning", *UNIPED (Tromsø)*, vol. 31, no. 3, pp. 32–45, 2008.

[LIE 10] LIEM A., "Planning and early implementation of vertical studio teaching based on a systems design approach", *Proceedings of the 12th International Conference on Engineering and Product Design Education "New Paradigms and Approaches"*, pp. 143–149, 2010.

[LIE 12a] LIE U., Framing an Eclectic Practice; Historical Models and Narratives of Product Design as Professional Work, Doctoral dissertation, Norwegian University of Science and Technology, Trondheim, 2012.

[LIE 12b] LIEM A., BRANGIER E., "Innovation and design approaches within prospective ergonomics", *Work: Journal of Prevention Assessment and Rehabilitation*, vol. 41, supplement 1, p. 5243, 2012.

[LIE 14a] LIEM A., "Toward prospective reasoning in design: an essay on relationships among designers' reasoning, business strategies, and innovation", *Le Travail Humain*, vol. 77, no. 1, pp. 91–102, 2014.

[LIE 14b] LIEM A., SIGURJONSSON J.B., "Positioning industrial design education within higher education: how to face increasingly challenging market forces?", *Uniped*, vol. 37, no. 2, pp. 44–57, 2014.

[LIJ 71] LIJPHART A., "Comparative politics and the comparative method", *American Political Science Review*, vol. 65, no. 3, pp. 682–693, 1971.

[LIN 85] LINCOLN Y.S., GUBA E.G., *Naturalistic Inquiry*, Sage Publications, Newbury Park, 1985.

[LUS 14] LUSKIN B.J., Industrial Ergonomics: Prevent Injury from Hand and Power Tool Use, available at: http://www.spineuniverse.com/wellness/ergonomics/industrial-ergonomics-prevent-injury-hand-power-tool-use, 2014.

[LYN 13] LYNDA, "Start Learning Today", available at: http://www.lynda.com/18B, 2013.

[MAG 11] MAGER B., SUNG T.J., "Special issue editorial: designing for services", *International Journal of Design*, vol. 5, no. 2, pp. 1–3, 2011.

[MAN 03] MANZINI E., VEZZOLI C., "A strategic design approach to develop sustainable product service systems: examples taken from the 'environmentally friendly innovation' Italian prize", *Journal of Cleaner Production*, vol. 11, no. 8, pp. 851–857, 2003.

[MAR 09] MARTIN R.L., *The Design of Business: Why Design Thinking is the Next Competitive Advantage*, Harvard Business Press, Boston, 2009.

[MAU 05] MAUBORGNE R., CHAN K.W., "Blue ocean strategy: from theory to practice", *California Management Review*, vol. 47, no. 3, pp. 105–122, 2005.

[MER 11] MERONI A., SANGIORGI D., *Design for Services*, Gower Publishing, Surrey, 2011.

[MEU 00] MEUTER M.L., OSTROM A.L., ROUNDTREE R.I. *et al.*, "Self-service technologies: understanding customer satisfaction with technology-based service encounters", *Journal of Marketing*, vol. 64, no. 3, pp. 50–64, 2000.

[MIC 08] MICHEL S., BROWN S.W., GALLAN A.S., "An expanded and strategic view of discontinuous innovations: deploying a service-dominant logic", *Journal of the Academy of Marketing Science*, vol. 36, no. 1, pp. 54–66, 2008.

[MIL 93] MILES I., "Services in the new industrial economy", *Futures*, vol. 25, no. 6, pp. 653–672, 1993.

[MIN 87] MINTZBERG H., *Crafting Strategy*, Harvard Business Review Press, Boston, 1987.

[MIN 85] MINTZBERG H., WATERS J.A., "Of strategies, deliberate and emergent", *Strategic Management Journal*, vol. 6, no. 3, pp. 257–272, 1985.

[MIN 89] MINTZBERG H., "Strategy Formation: Ten Schools of Thought", in FREDRICKSON J. (ed.), *Perspectus on Strategic Management*, Ballinger, New York, 1989.

[MON 67] MONTMOLLIN M., *Les Systémes Homme-Machine*, PUF, Paris, 1967.

[MOO 96] MOORE J.S., GARG A., "Use of participatory ergonomics teams to address musculoskeletal hazards in the red meat packing industry", *American Journal of Industrial Medicine*, vol. 29, no. 4, pp. 402–408, 1996.

[MOR 95] MORAY N., "Ergonomics and the global problems of the twenty-first century", *Ergonomics*, vol. 38, no. 8, pp. 1691–1707, 1995.

[MOR 00] MORAY N., "Culture, politics and ergonomics", *Ergonomics*, vol. 43, no. 7, pp. 858–868, 2000.

[MOR 05] MORITZ S., *Service Design, Practical Access to an Evolving Field*, Köln International School of Design, London, 2005.

[MØR 11] MØRK S.K., "Innovation through design: Epistemological relations between innovation strategies and philosophies in the design process", in BAGGERUD B., BOKS C. (eds), *TPD4505 Design Theory, Article Collection, Spring/Autumn*, pp. 209–222, NTNU, 2011.

[NAG 07] NAG R., HAMBRICK D.C., CHEN M., "What is strategic management, really? Inductive derivation of a consensus definition of the field", *Strategic Management Journal*, vol. 28, pp. 935–955, 2007.

[NEL 12] NELSON J., BUISINE S., AOUSSAT A., "A methodological proposal to assist scenario-based design in the early stages of innovation projects", *Le Travail Humain*, vol. 75, no. 3, pp. 279–305, 2012.

[NEL 14] NELSON J., BUISINE S., AOUSSAT A. *et al.*, "Generating prospective scenarios of use in innovation projects", *Le Travail Humain*, vol. 77, no. 1, pp. 21–38, 2014.

[NEM 04] NEMETH C., *Human Factors Methods for Design*, CRC Press, Boca Raton, 2004.

[NIE 01] NIEDERHELMAN M., "Education through design", *Design Issues*, vol. 17, no. 3, pp. 83–87, 2001.

[NIE 99] NIELSEN J., *Designing Web Usability: The Practice of Simplicity*, New Riders Publishing, 1999.

[NOB 93] NOBLET J., *Industrial Design*, A.F.A.A., Paris, 1993.

[NOR 10] NORMAN D., *Invited talk for the 30th anniversary of the Human-Systems Integration Board of the National Research Council*, the National Academies, Washington, DC, available at: http://www.jnd.org/dn.mss/why_human_systems_in.html, December 2, 2010.

[NOR 14] NORMAN D.A., VERGANTI R., "Incremental and radical innovation: Design research vs. technology and meaning change", *Design Issues*, vol. 30, no. 1, pp. 78–96, 2014.

[NOR 91] NORO K., IMADA A.S., *Participatory Ergonomics*, Taylor and Francis, London, 1991.

[NOR 10] NORROS L., "Developing human factors/ergonomics as a design discipline", *Applied Ergonomics*, vol. 45, no. 1, pp. 61–71, 2014.

[NRC 01] NATIONAL RESEARCH COUNCIL (NRC), *Musculoskeletal Disorders and the Workplace: Low Back and Upper Extremities*, National Academy Press, Washington, DC, 2001.

[OUD 11] DEN OUDEN E., *Innovation Design: Creating Value for People, Organizations and Society*, Springer Science & Business Media, London, 2011.

[OWE 95] OWEN B.D., KEENE K., OLSON S. *et al.*, "An ergonomic approach to reducing back stress while carrying out patient handling tasks with a hospitalized patient", in HAGBERG H., STOBEL W. (eds), *Occupational Health for Health Care Workers*, ECOMED, Landsber, 1995.

[PAR 97] PARASURAMAN R., RILEY V., "Humans and automation: Use, misuse, disuse, abuse", *Human Factors: The Journal of the Human Factors and Ergonomics Society*, vol. 39, no. 2, pp. 230–253, Landsber, 1997.

[PAR 06] PARKER S., HEAPY J., *The Journey to the Interface*, Demos, London, 2006.

[PAT 12] PATEL H., PETTITT M., WILSON J. R., "Factors of collaborative working: A framework for a collaboration model", *Applied Ergonomics*, vol. 43, no. 1, pp. 1–26, 2012.

[PAV 07] PAVAGEAU P., NASCIMENTO A., FALZON P., "Les risques d'exclusion dans un contexte de transformation organisationnelle", *Perspectives Interdisciplinaires sur Le Travail et La Santé*, vol. 9, no. 2, pp. 2–17, 2007.

[PER 83] PERROW C., "The organizational context of human factors engineering", *Administrative Science Quarterly*, vol. 28, no. 4, pp. 521–541, 1983.

[PET 88] PETTIGREW A., "Longitudinal field research on change: theory and practice", *Paper Presented at the National Science Foundation Conference on Longitudinal Research Methods in Organisations*, Austin, 1988.

[PFE 10] PFEFFER J., "Building sustainable organizations: The human factor", *The Academy of Management Perspectives*, vol. 24, no. 1, pp 34–45, 2010.

[PHE 86] PHEASANT S., *Bodyspace: Anthropometry, Ergonomics and Design*, Taylor & Francis, London, 1986.

[PHI 00] PHILLIPS D.C., BURBULES N.C., *Post-positivism and Educational Research*, Rowman & Littlefield, Maryland, 2000.

[PHO 15] PHOTIADIS T., SOULELES N., "The influences of user experience, aesthetics and psychology in the design process of 3D avatars (theoretical model)", *Journal for Virtual Worlds Research*, vol. 8, no. 1, 2015.

[PIN 86] PINFIELD L.T., "A field evaluation of perspectives on organizational decision making", *Administrative Science Quarterly*, vol. 31, no. 3, pp. 365–388, 1986.

[POR 85] PORTER M.E., *Competitive Strategy: Creating and Sustaining Superior Performance*, Free Press, New York, 1985.

[PRA 90] PRAHALAD C.K., HAMEL G., *The Core Competence of The Corporation*, Harvard Business Review, 1990.

[PRA 00] PRAHALAD C.K., RAMASWAMY V., "Co-opting Customer Competence", *Harvard Business Review*, January–February, pp. 79–87, 2000.

[PRA 10] PRAHALAD D., SAWHNEY R., *Predictable magic: unleash the power of design strategy to transform your business*, Pearson Prentice Hall, New Jersey, 2010.

[PRE 03] PRESS M., COOPER R., *The design experience: the role of design and designers in the twenty-first century*, Ashgate Publishing, 2003.

[PUE 12] PUENTES R., Have Americans Hit Peak Travel? A discussion of the changes on US driving habits, IFT discussion paper 2012-14, Brookings Institute, 2012.

[RAM 07] RAMAKANTAN R., "The discussion in a research paper", *Indian Journal of Radiology and Imaging*, vol. 17, no. 3, p. 148, 2007.

[RAM 11] RAMPINO L., "The innovation pyramid: a categorization of the innovation phenomenon in the product-design field", *International Journal of Design*, vol. 5, no. 1, pp. 3–16, 2011.

[RAS 00] RASMUSSEN J., "Human factors in a dynamic information society: where are we heading?", *Ergonomics*, vol. 43, no. 7, pp. 869–879, 2000.

[REA 99] REASON J., *Managing the Risk of Organizational Accidents*, Ashgate, Aldershot, 1999.

[RIT 73] RITTEL H.W.J., WEBBER M.M., "Dilemmas in a General Theory of Planning", *Policy Sciences*, vol. 4, no. 2, pp. 155–169, 1973.

[ROB 09] ROBERT J.M., BRANGIER E., "What Is Prospective Ergonomics? A Reflection and a Position on the Future of Ergonomics", in KARSH B.-T. (ed.), *Ergonomics and Health Aspects, HCII 2009, LNCS 5624*, Springer-Verlag, Berlin-Heidelberg, 2009.

[ROB 12] ROBERT J.M., BRANGIER E., "Prospective ergonomics: origin, goal, and prospects", *Work*, vol. 41, supplement 1, pp. 5235–5242, 2012.

[ROB 01] ROBERTSON M.M., "Macroergonomics: A work system design perspective", *Proceedings of the SELF-ACE 2001 Conference–Ergonomics for Changing Work*, Montreal, Canada, 2001.

[ROO 95] ROOZENBURG N.F., EEKELS J., *Product Design: Fundamentals and Methods*, Chichester, John Wiley & Sons, vol. 2, 1995.

[ROR 90] RORTY R., "Pragmatism as anti-representationalism", in MURPHY J.P., *Pragmatism : From Pierce to Davidson*, Westview Press, Boulder, pp. 1–6, 1990.

[ROS 83] ROSENBROCK H.H., "Flexible manufacturing systems in which the operator is not subservient to the machine", *Research Project Mimeo*, 2nd edition, UMIST, UK, 1983.

[ROS 09] ROSSON M.B., CARROLL J.M., "Scenario-based design", in SEARS A., JACKO J. (eds), *Human-Computer Interaction*, Development Process, Boca Raton, CRC Press, 2009.

[ROT 99] ROTH S., "The State of Design Research", *Design Issues*, vol. 15, no. 2, pp. 18–26, 1999.

[ROU 06] ROUBELAT F., "Scenarios to challenge strategic paradigms: lessons from 2025", *Futures*, vol. 38, no. 5, pp. 519–527, 2006.

[ROU 91] ROUSSEL R.A., SAAD K.N., ERICKSON T.J., *Third generation R&D: managing the link to corporate strategy*, Harvard Business Press, Boston, 1991.

[SAM 05] SAMARAS G.M., HORST R.L., "A systems engineering perspective on the human-centered design of health information systems", *Journal of Biomedical Information*, vol. 38, no. 1, pp. 61–74, 2005.

[SAN 96] SANDELOWSKI M., "One is the liveliest number: the case orientation of qualitative research", *Research in Nursing & Health*, vol. 19, no. 6, pp. 525–529, 1996.

[SAN 08a] SANDERS E.B.-N., "On modeling: an evolving map of design practice and design research", *Interactions*, vol. 15, no. 6, pp. 13–17, 2008.

[SAN 08b] SANDERS E.B.-N., STAPPERS P.J., "Co-creation and the new landscapes of design", *Co-design*, vol. 4, no. 1, pp. 5–18, 2008.

[SCH 87] SCHÖN D.A., *Educating the Reflective Practitioner, Toward a New Design for Teaching and Learning in the Professions*, Jossey-Bass Publishers, San Francisco, 1987.

[SCH 95] SCHÖN D.A., *The Reflective Practitioner, How Professionals Think in Action*, 2nd edition, Arena, Aldershot, 1995.

[SCH 09] SCHLICK C.M., "Editorial: A Festschrift in Honor of Professor Doktor-Ingenieur Holger Luczak", in SCHLICK C.M., *Industrial Engineering and Ergonomics – Vision, Concepts, Methods and Tools*, pp. xi–xli, Springer, Berlin, 2009.

[SCO 98] SCOTT P., "Massification, internationalisation and globalisation", in SCOTT P., *The Globalization of Higher Education*, SRHE & Open University Press, Buckingham, 1998.

[SEN 09] SEN A.K., *The Idea of Justice*, Allen Lane, London/New York, 2009.

[SET 01] SETHIA N.K., "Generating and exploiting interdisciplinary knowledge in design product development and innovation in the new economy", *The 2001 IDSA National Education Conference,* Boston, 2001.

[SHE 06] SHEN S.T., WOOLLEY M., PRIOR S., "Towards culture-centred design", *Interacting with Computers,* vol. 18, no. 4, pp. 820–852, 2006.

[SIG 10] SIGURJONSSON J.B., HOLGERSEN T.D., "What do they do? A survey of employment and work situation for "IDE" candidates", *Proceedings of the 12th International Conference on Engineering and Product Design Education "NEW PARADIGMS AND APPROACHES",* Trondheim, 2010.

[SIM 96] SIMON H.A., *The Sciences of the Artificial,* 3rd edition, MIT Press, Cambridge, 1996.

[SIM 09] SIMONS H., *Case Study Research in Practice,* Sage Publications, London, 2009.

[SIN 94] SINGLETON W.T., "From research to practice, a personal view: are researchers producing work that's usable in system design? Maybe not", *Ergonomics in Design,* vol. 2, no. 3, pp. 30–34, 1994.

[SLO 63] SLOAN A.P., *My Years with General Motors,* Doubleday, New York, 1963.

[SNO 92] SNODGRASS A., COYNE R., "Models, metaphors, and the hermeneutics of designing", *Design Issues,* vol. 9, no. 1, pp. 56–74, 1992.

[SO 14] SO R.H.Y., LAM S.T., "Factors affecting the appreciation generated through applying human factors/ergonomics (HFE) principles to systems of work", *Applied Ergonomics,* vol. 45, no. 1, pp. 99–109, 2014.

[SON 12] SONDEREGGER A., ZBINDEN G., UEBELBACHER A., "The influence of product aesthetics and usability over the course of time: a longitudinal field experiment", *Ergonomics,* vol. 55, no. 7, pp. 713–730, 2012.

[STA 88] STALK G., "Time - The Next Source of Competitive Advantage", *Harvard Business Review,* vol. 66, pp. 41–51, 1988.

[STA 97] STANTON N.A., *Human Factors in Consumer Products,* CRC Press, Boca Raton, 1997.

[STI 10] STICKDORN M., SCHNEIDER J., *This is service design thinking: basics-tools-cases,* BIS Publishers, Amsterdam, 2010.

[SUK 11] SUKHOCHEV A., Technology Transfer: Turning Knowledge into Value, Case study, 2011.

[SWA 02] SWANN C., "Nellie is dead", *Art Design and Communication in Higher Education,* vol. 1, no. 1, pp. 50–55, 2002.

[SWE 87] SWEDBERG R., HIMMELSTRAND U., BRULIN G., "The paradigm of economic sociology", *Theory and Society,* vol. 16, no. 1, pp. 169–213, 1987.

[TEE 97] TEECE D.J., PISANO G., SHUEN A., "Dynamic capabilities and strategic management", *Strategic Management Journal*, vol. 18, no. 7, p. 509, 1997.

[TEE 07] TEECE D.J., "Explicating dynamic capabilities: the nature and microfoundations of (sustainable) enterprise performance", *Strategic Management Journal*, vol. 28, no. 13, pp. 1319–1350, 2007.

[TEE 10] TEECE D.J., "Business models, business strategy and innovation", *Long Range Planning*, vol. 43, no. 2, pp. 172–194, 2010.

[THO 11] THOMAS G., "A typology for the case study in social science following a review of definition, discourse, and structure", *Qualitative Inquiry*, vol. 17, no. 6, pp. 511–521, 2011.

[TJØ 10] TJØRVE K.M.C., SUTTERUD E., MIDTSKOGEN B. *et al.* "The use of technology in teaching: student satisfaction and perceived learning", *Uniped*, vol. 33, no. 3, pp. 56–64, 2010.

[TRA 09] TRATHEN S., VARADARAJAN S., "Taking on Australian Industrial Design Education: Current Practice and Future", in CLARKE A., HOGARTH P., ION B. *et al.* (eds), *Creating a Better World: Proceedings for the 11th Engineering and Product Design International Conference*, Brighton, 2009.

[TSO 96] TSOUKAS H., "The firm as a distributed knowledge system: a constructionist approach", *Strategic Management Journal*, vol. 17, issue S2, pp. 11–25, 1996.

[TUR 12] TURCOTTE M., "Profile of seniors' transportation habits", *Canadian Social Trends*, vol. 93, 11-008-X, pp. 1–16, 2012.

[ULL 12] ULLAH A.S., RASHID M.M., TAMAKI J., "On some unique features of C–K theory of design", *CIRP Journal of Manufacturing Science and Technology*, vol. 5, no. 1, pp. 55–66, 2012.

[UNI 15] UNITED STATES DEPARTMENT OF LABOR, Occupation Safety and Health Administration: Prevention of Musculoskeletal Disorders in the Workplace, Report, available at: https://www.osha.gov/SLTC/ergonomics/, 2015.

[VAN 08] VAN ROMPAY T.J.L., "Product expression: Bridging the gap between the symbolic and the concrete", in SCHIFFERSTEIN H.N.J., HEKKERT P. (eds.), *Product Experience*, Elsevier, Amsterdam, 2008.

[VAR 08] VARGO S.L., LUSCH R.F., "Service-dominant logic: continuing the evolution", *Journal of the Academy of Marketing Science*, vol. 36, no. 1, pp. 1–10, 2008.

[VER 08] VERGANTI R., "Design, meanings, and radical innovation: a metamodel and a research agenda", *Journal of Product Innovation Management*, vol. 25, no. 5, pp. 436–456, 2008.

[VER 11] VERGANTI R., "Radical design and technology epiphanies: a new focus for research on design management", *Journal of Product Innovation Management*, vol. 28, no. 3, pp. 384–388, 2011.

[VER 13] VERGANTI R., ÖBERG Å., "Interpreting and envisioning—a hermeneutic framework to look at radical innovation of meanings", *Industrial Marketing Management*, vol. 42, no. 1, pp. 86–95, 2013.

[VER 05] VERYZER R.W., BORJA DE MOZOTA B., "The Impact of User-Oriented Design on New Product Development: an Examination of Fundamental Relationships", *Journal of Product Innovation Management*, vol. 22, no. 2, pp. 128–143, 2005.

[VIC 99] VICENTE K.J., *Cognitive Work Analysis: Towards Safe, Productive, and Healthy Computer-Based Work*, Lawrence Erlbaum Associates, Mahwah, NJ, 1999.

[VON 86] VON HIPPEL E., "Lead users: a source of novel product concepts"; *Management Science*, vol. 32, no. 7, pp. 791–805, 1986.

[WAL 13] WALDROP M., "Massive Open Online Courses, aka MOOCs, Transform Higher Education and Science", Scientific American, available at: http://www.scientificamerican.com/article.cfm?id =massive-open-online-courses-transform-higher-education-and-science, 2013.

[WEI 99] WEICK K.E., QUINN R.E., "Organizational change and development", *Annual Review of Psychology*, vol. 50, no. 1, pp. 361–386, 1999.

[WEN 00] WENGER E., "Communities of practice and social learning systems", *Organisation Articles*, vol. 7, no. 2, pp. 225–246, 2000.

[WER 84] WERNERFELT B., "A resource-based view of the firm", *Strategic Management Journal*, vol. 5, no. 2, pp. 171–180, 1984.

[WHI 92] WHITTINGTON R., "Putting Giddens into action: social systems and managerial agency", *Journal of Management Studies*, vol. 29, no. 6, pp. 693–712, 1992.

[WHI 01] WHITTINGTON R., *"What is Strategy – and does it matter"*, 2nd editon, Cengage Learning EMEA, UK, 2001.

[WIL 91] WILLIAMS R.J.P., "Science in universities: teaching, research and autonomy", *Studies in Higher Education*, vol. 16, no. 1, pp. 15–22, 1991.

[WIL 00] WILSON J.R., "Fundamentals of ergonomics in theory and practice", *Applied Ergonomics*, vol. 31, no. 6, pp. 557–567, 2000.

[WIL 14] WILSON J.R., CARAYON P., "Systems ergonomics: Looking into the future – Editorial for special issue on systems ergonomics/human factors", *Applied Ergonomics*, vol. 1, no. 45, pp. 3–4, 2014.

[WIL 09] WILSON J.R., RYAN B., SCHOCK A. *et al.*, "Understanding safety and production risks in rail engineering planning and protection", *Ergonomics*, vol. 52, no. 7, pp. 774–790, 2009.

[WOO 00] WOODS D., DEKKER S., "Anticipating the effects of technological change: a new era of dynamics for human factors", *Theoretical Issues in Ergonomics Science*, vol. 1, no. 3, pp. 272–282, 2000.

[YAN 05] YANG M.-Y., YOU M., CHEN F.-C., "Competencies and qualifications for industrial design jobs: implications for design practice, education and student career guidance", *Design Studies*, vol. 26, no. 2, pp. 155–189, 2005.

[YIN 84] YIN R.K., *Case Study Research*, Sage, Beverly Hills, 1984.

[ZIN 05] ZINK K.J., "From industrial safety to corporate health management", *Ergonomics*, vol. 48, no. 5, pp. 534–546, 2005.

[ZIN 14] ZINK K.J., "Designing sustainable work systems: the need for a systems approach", *Applied Ergonomics*, vol. 45, no. 1, pp. 126–132, 2014.

Index

Other titles from

in

Information Systems, Web and Pervasive Computing

2017

LESAS Anne-Marie, MIRANDA Serge
The Art and Science of NFC Programming
(Intellectual Technologies Set – Volume 3)

SZONIECKY Samuel, BOUHAÏ Nasreddine
Collective Intelligence and Digital Archives: Towards Knowledge
Ecosystems
(Digital Tools and Uses Set – Volume 1)

REYES-GARCIA Everardo, BOUHAÏ Nasreddine
Designing Interactive Hypermedia Systems
(Digital Tools and Uses Set – Volume 2)

2016

BEN CHOUIKHA Mona
Organizational Design for Knowledge Management

BERTOLO David
Interactions on Digital Tablets in the Context of 3D Geometry Learning
(Human-Machine Interaction Set – Volume 2)

BOUVARD Patricia, SUZANNE Hervé
Collective Intelligence Development in Business

DAUPHINÉ André
Geographical Models in Mathematica

EL FALLAH SEGHROUCHNI Amal, ISHIKAWA Fuyuki, HÉRAULT Laurent, TOKUDA Hideyuki
Enablers for Smart Cities

FABRE Renaud, in collaboration with MESSERSCHMIDT-MARIET Quentin, HOLVOET Margot
New Challenges for Knowledge

GAUDIELLO Ilaria, ZIBETTI Elisabetta
Learning Robotics, with Robotics, by Robotics
(Human-Machine Interaction Set – Volume 3)

HENROTIN Joseph
The Art of War in the Network Age
(Intellectual Technologies Set – Volume 1)

KITAJIMA Munéo
Memory and Action Selection in Human–Machine Interaction
(Human–Machine Interaction Set – Volume 1)

LAGRAÑA Fernando
E-mail and Behavioral Changes: Uses and Misuses of Electronic Communications

LEIGNEL Jean-Louis, UNGARO Thierry, STAAR Adrien
Digital Transformation

NOYER Jean-Max
Transformation of Collective Intelligences
(Intellectual Technologies Set – Volume 2)

VENTRE Daniel
Information Warfare – 2nd edition

VITALIS André
The Uncertain Digital Revolution

KEMBELLEC Gérald, CHARTRON Ghislaine, SALEH Imad
Recommender Systems

MATHIAN Hélène, SANDERS Lena
Spatio-temporal Approaches: Geographic Objects and Change Process

PLANTIN Jean-Christophe
Participatory Mapping

VENTRE Daniel
Chinese Cybersecurity and Defense

2013

BERNIK Igor
Cybercrime and Cyberwarfare

CAPET Philippe, DELAVALLADE Thomas
Information Evaluation

LEBRATY Jean-Fabrice, LOBRE-LEBRATY Katia
Crowdsourcing: One Step Beyond

SALLABERRY Christian
Geographical Information Retrieval in Textual Corpora

2012

BUCHER Bénédicte, LE BER Florence
Innovative Software Development in GIS

GAUSSIER Eric, YVON François
Textual Information Access

STOCKINGER Peter
Audiovisual Archives: Digital Text and Discourse Analysis

VENTRE Daniel
Cyber Conflict

2011

BANOS Arnaud, THÉVENIN Thomas
Geographical Information and Urban Transport Systems

DAUPHINÉ André
Fractal Geography

LEMBERGER Pirmin, MOREL Mederic
Managing Complexity of Information Systems

STOCKINGER Peter
Introduction to Audiovisual Archives

STOCKINGER Peter
Digital Audiovisual Archives

VENTRE Daniel
Cyberwar and Information Warfare

2010

BONNET Pierre
Enterprise Data Governance

BRUNET Roger
Sustainable Geography

CARREGA Pierre
Geographical Information and Climatology

CAUVIN Colette, ESCOBAR Francisco, SERRADJ Aziz
Thematic Cartography – 3-volume series
Thematic Cartography and Transformations – Volume 1
Cartography and the Impact of the Quantitative Revolution – Volume 2
New Approaches in Thematic Cartography – Volume 3

LANGLOIS Patrice
Simulation of Complex Systems in GIS

MATHIS Philippe
Graphs and Networks – 2nd edition

THERIAULT Marius, DES ROSIERS François
Modeling Urban Dynamics

2009

BONNET Pierre, DETAVERNIER Jean-Michel, VAUQUIER Dominique
Sustainable IT Architecture: the Progressive Way of Overhauling Information Systems with SOA

PAPY Fabrice
Information Science

RIVARD François, ABOU HARB Georges, MERET Philippe
The Transverse Information System

ROCHE Stéphane, CARON Claude
Organizational Facets of GIS

2008

BRUGNOT Gérard
Spatial Management of Risks

FINKE Gerd
Operations Research and Networks

GUERMOND Yves
Modeling Process in Geography

KANEVSKI Michael
Advanced Mapping of Environmental Data

MANOUVRIER Bernard, LAURENT Ménard
Application Integration: EAI, B2B, BPM and SOA

PAPY Fabrice
Digital Libraries

2007

DOBESCH Hartwig, DUMOLARD Pierre, DYRAS Izabela
Spatial Interpolation for Climate Data

SANDERS Lena
Models in Spatial Analysis

2006

CLIQUET Gérard
Geomarketing

CORNIOU Jean-Pierre
Looking Back and Going Forward in IT

DEVILLERS Rodolphe, JEANSOULIN Robert
Fundamentals of Spatial Data Quality

Printed and bound by CPI Group (UK) Ltd, Croydon, CR0 4YY